s t o r i e s
of
PRAYER
for a
h e a l t h y
SOUL

This special edition is published by the
Billy Graham Evangelistic Association with
permission from Zondervan Publi...

D0057298

Stories of Prayer for a Healthy Soul

Copyright 2000 by Christine M. Anderson

ISBN 1–59328–009–2

All Scripture quotations, unless otherwise noted, are taken from the Holy Bible, New International Version (North American Edition), Copyright 1973, 1978 1984 by International Bible Society. Used by permission of ZondervanPublishingHouse. All rights reserved.

The "NIV" and "New International Version" trademarks are registered in the United States Patent and Trademark Office by International Bible Society.

Requests for information should be addressed to:
        Inspirio, the Gift Group of Zondervan
        Grand Rapids, Michigan 49530

Compiler: Christine M. Anderson
Associate Editor: Molly Detweiler
Design Manager: Amy E. Langeler
Design: Mark Veldheer
Cover photograph © Corbis Images
Interior photography by Corbis Images, Photodisc, Comstock, and Eyewire

stories
of
PRAYER
for a
healthy
SOUL

Compiled by

Christine M. Anderson

inspirio

The gift group of Zondervan

CONTENTS

$\mathcal{P}$rayer digs the channels from the

reservoir of God's boundless

resources to the tiny pools of our lives.

E. STANLEY JONES

PRAYER
that
PROVIDES

Listen to my cry, for I am in desperate need.

Psalm 142:6

BRADY'S BIRTHDAY

Jennifer Smith-Morris

GOD'S WORD

> The LORD is gracious and righteous;
>> our God is full of compassion.
> The LORD protects the simplehearted;
>> when I was in great need, he saved me.
> Be at rest once more, O my soul,
>> for the LORD has been good to you.

Psalm 116:5–7

RECENTLY, WHEN MY FIRSTBORN turned seven, I found myself thinking back to his birth. It was the first time I experienced the power of prayer.

I was twenty, recently married, unexpectedly pregnant, and new to Christianity. I went into labor at seven months. Medication stopped the contractions and I was taken by ambulance to a hospital equipped to care for premature babies. Brady was born one week later.

During those first blurry hours, we learned that he had an infection and a heart murmur. Sometimes his heart would stop and he would stop breathing. There were tubes and wires everywhere and alarms sounded if something was wrong. It was an overwhelming introduction to motherhood.

The day after Brady's birth, the doctor discharged me. We were eighty miles from home. While I had been in the hospital, my husband, Andy, drove each evening to be with me, stayed the night in my room, then drove home the next morning for classes and work. Now we had no place to stay.

There was a Ronald McDonald House nearby where parents of hospitalized children could stay. For only ten dollars a night, we could have a room for as long as we needed it and kitchen facilities. There

were no openings, so we placed our names on the waiting list. The hospital had two family rooms for brief stays. Although they cost twice as much, they offered short-term solutions for families. Unfortunately, they, too, were booked. I had no car, only twenty dollars, and no credit card. We couldn't have afforded a hotel even if one had been nearby.

Brady's heart stopped twice that day. He had no sucking reflex and was fed through a stomach tube. He developed jaundice and began light therapy. All around alarms sounded and nurses bustled about. I sat next to his incubator and watched him breathe. I didn't want to look away for fear he would stop.

By that afternoon I had called the Ronald McDonald House three times to see if there was an opening. There wasn't. Taking a break, I walked outside the hospital, sat on the steps, and began to cry. My baby was sick, my body was weak, my husband was driving eighty miles in bad weather, and we had no place to sleep. It was too much.

A woman approached me. "Can I help you?" she asked.

I choked out my circumstances. I told her about Brady's heart stopping and how we had no place to stay.

"I'll pray for you," she said, and she put her hand on my shoulder. "My daughter is having a baby, too. There are complications." The baby's kidneys were failing and his life was in danger.

After she left, I felt humbled that she took the time to

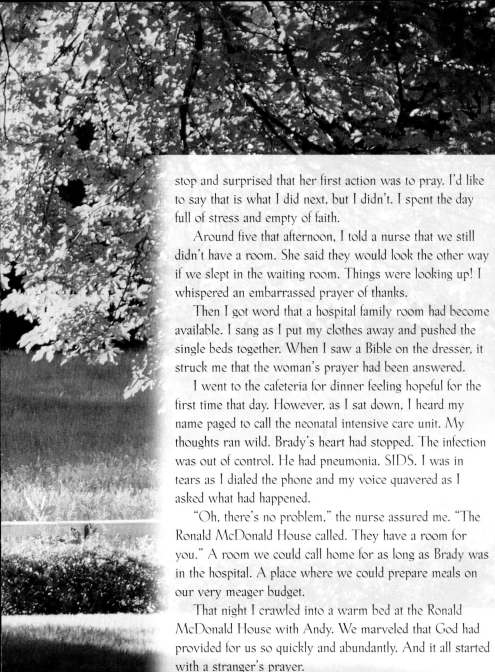

stop and surprised that her first action was to pray. I'd like to say that is what I did next, but I didn't. I spent the day full of stress and empty of faith.

Around five that afternoon, I told a nurse that we still didn't have a room. She said they would look the other way if we slept in the waiting room. Things were looking up! I whispered an embarrassed prayer of thanks.

Then I got word that a hospital family room had become available. I sang as I put my clothes away and pushed the single beds together. When I saw a Bible on the dresser, it struck me that the woman's prayer had been answered.

I went to the cafeteria for dinner feeling hopeful for the first time that day. However, as I sat down, I heard my name paged to call the neonatal intensive care unit. My thoughts ran wild. Brady's heart had stopped. The infection was out of control. He had pneumonia. SIDS. I was in tears as I dialed the phone and my voice quavered as I asked what had happened.

"Oh, there's no problem," the nurse assured me. "The Ronald McDonald House called. They have a room for you." A room we could call home for as long as Brady was in the hospital. A place where we could prepare meals on our very meager budget.

That night I crawled into a warm bed at the Ronald McDonald House with Andy. We marveled that God had provided for us so quickly and abundantly. And it all started with a stranger's prayer.

WORDS OF WISDOM

God says to us, "Pray, because I have all kinds of things for you; and when you ask, you will receive. I have all this grace, and you live with scarcity. Come unto me, all you who labor. Why are you so rushed? Where are you running now? Everything you need, I have."

Jim Cymbala

GOD'S PROMISE

The LORD is good,
    a refuge in times of trouble.
He cares for those who trust in him.

Nahum 1:7

PRAYER

Lord, I have been so defeated by circumstances. I have felt like an animal trapped in a corner with nowhere to flee. Where are you in all this, Lord? The night is dark. I cannot feel your presence.

Help me to know that the darkness is really Shade of your hand, outstretched caressingly; that the "hemming in" is your doing. Perhaps there was no other way you could get my full attention, no other way I would allow you to demonstrate what you can do in my life.

I see now that the emptier my cup is, the more space there is to receive your love and supply.

Catherine Marshall

WILDERNESS PRAYER
Lee Maynard

GOD'S WORD

> Some trust in chariots and some in horses,
>> but we trust in the name of the LORD our God.

Psalm 20:7

IT WAS 1978. In the early hours, when the tops of trees were still lost in darkness, I parked my truck and stepped into New Mexico's Gila Wilderness. My plan was to hike twenty miles in, then join up with a group of nine Outward Bound School students and their instructors, a "patrol." I was the school director, and I was worried about this patrol: three New England preppies, a college freshman, three high school graduates from Dallas, and two South Chicago street kids who had been sentenced to Outward Bound in lieu of jail.

I looked forward to hiking in the Gila. Even after half a lifetime spent outdoors, I couldn't seem to see it enough. But it was midsummer, and the sun's heat poured down relentlessly. At midday I stopped, drank some water, and for the first time noticed the heat in my boots. The boots were not new. I had worn them for some weeks and thought they were ready for the Gila. I was wrong.

I reached camp in the middle of the evening meal, took off my boots and socks, and padded around on the soft forest floor. I inspected my feet and counted eleven blisters, near blisters, and hot spots. Still, I told no one about my problem.

We sat and talked for hours. After two weeks in the wilderness, only one student, a New Englander, seemed disenchanted with the course. He had tried to quit but had been talked out of it by the staff. In the morning, the New Englander was gone. He had left hours before, thrashing back down the trail I'd come in on. We couldn't just let him go into the unforgiving wilderness. Since I was the extra man, I put on the devil boots and went after him.

I soon realized I wasn't just limping any more—I was walking as though barefoot on hot glass. As I shuffled and stumbled, I tried to keep my mind above my ankles. A new sound sucked its way into my consciousness, and I realized it was coming

from my boots. I sat on a fallen tree, held my feet out in front of me, and looked at the crimson oozing from the eyelets. If I took the boots off, I would never get them on again.

Eventually the trail came out of the brush and straight into the Gila River, flowing down from the high country through shaded canyons. By the time it got to me, this narrow, shallow river was still icy, and I couldn't wait to feel it against my baking feet. But when the water poured into my boots, the burning sensation was replaced with a thousand stabs that seemed to puncture every blister. My scream cut through the canyon, and I went face forward into the water. Then I got up and staggered across the river.

Since there was no rational solution to my problem, my mind began to create irrational ones. The answer, obviously, was . . . a horse. If I just had a horse, my feet would no longer be a problem, and I could catch the New Englander. Like King Richard III, I began to implore, "Give me another horse! Have mercy!" What was the next word? Oh yes. "Jesu."

The sun was low against my back, and my shadow reached far down the stony trail. I would never get to the end of my shadow. And then I stopped. The right shoulder of my shadow moved, a bulging darkness down on the trail. A huge mass, motionless now, blocked most of the low sun, an elongated head bobbing up in attention to my presence. It was a horse. A ghost born of pain. It was a beautiful ghost, but I would have to make it go away. So I confronted it directly, dragging myself right up to the horse and grabbing its halter.

It was a real horse.

The animal had a halter and a lead rope but no saddle. Something was going on here that I didn't understand, but I was not going to question it. I gathered up the lead rope and struggled onto the horse's back. "A horse, a horse," I mumbled as it calmly carried me down the trail and into the falling darkness. "Jesu."

The horse walked through the night and did not stop until we got to the trail-head, where I found the New Englander sitting on the bumper of my truck. I took off the hated boots, bandaged my feet, and hobbled the horse to a patch of grass. The New Englander and I slept nearby.

At first light two wranglers showed up looking for the horse. They said it had never wandered off before and didn't know why it did this time. They said the horse's name was King.

WORDS OF WISDOM

Prayer can obtain everything; can open the windows of heaven and shut the gates of hell; can put a holy constraint upon God, and detain an angel till he leave a blessing; can open the treasures of rain and soften the iron ribs of rocks till they melt into a flowing river; can arrest the sun in his course, and send the winds upon our errands.

Jeremy Taylor

GOD'S PROMISE

Your Father knows what you need before you ask him.

Matthew 6:8

PRAYER

Lord, my faith is no faith at all if it depends upon whether or not you perform a miracle for me or for someone I love. And yet I believe that miracles do happen. So I ask you to look with compassion on my prayer and to grant the desires of my heart. Whether your answer is yes or no, now or later, I trust that you hear me, that you understand my distress, and that you will act with compassion. Amen.

Ann Spangler

KEVIN'S DELIVERANCE
William Hanford

GOD'S WORD

The apostles said to the Lord, "Increase our faith!"

Luke 17:5

THE BRILLIANT SUNSHINE of the June day could not penetrate the heavy cloud that hovered over my wife and me. We had just discovered that many miles away, our son had been seduced into a cult.

Friends, coworkers, and my wife, Carolyn, urged me to fly immediately to where Kevin was. They exhorted me to forcibly bring him home. Kevin, however, was an adult, and we had no legal authority over him. My heart instinctively knew that such a trip would be futile.

What was left for us to do? We prayed, all the while urged by friends and family to go and extract our son from the cult. Earnestly I sought God's guidance. Should I go, or should I stay home and pray? As the days dragged on, I grew more and more convicted that we were to depend on God through prayer alone.

Throughout each day, Carolyn and I reached out to God for Kevin—in the car, at work, together in the evening. We pled for his deliverance from the darkness in which he was enveloped through the false teachings of the cult. Each night, we would commit our son into the hands of God and then retire. Carolyn, however, would often lay awake for hours, plagued by a mixture of hope and helplessness.

One evening as we lay on our bed reading our Bibles, I struck a vein of gold in Romans 8. Newly encouraged by its familiar truths, I read the entire chapter aloud to Carolyn, emphasizing verse 28, "And we know that in all things God works for the good of those who love him, who have been called according to his purpose." When I finished reading, she said tearfully, "Read it again!" Once again, we drank in the uplifting truths of that power-packed chapter. Then we prayed and turned out the lights.

Another night, as I was reading from Mark 9, the verses about Jesus' healing of a boy caught my attention. I read and reread Mark 9:14–29. In this passage, a father brings his afflicted son to Jesus with these words: "If you can do anything, take pity on us and help us."

"If you can?" said Jesus. "Everything is possible for him who believes."

The desperate father quickly replied, "I do believe; help me overcome my unbelief!" With that, Jesus healed the boy.

The disciples had tried to heal the boy before Jesus arrived on the scene. When they asked Jesus why they were not able to heal him, Jesus explained, "This kind can come out only by prayer."

My heart leaped within me. That's it! Kevin will come out of the cult only by prayer! I read the passage to Carolyn. I confessed, "We've been praying desperately, but it's been mixed with unbelief, as though we were praying, 'Lord, if You can . . .' We need to pray and *believe*."

Carolyn took the Bible from me and read the story for herself. With tears in her eyes, she handed the Bible back to me and said, "Write in the margin of that passage, 'We believe!'" I did so and added the date and Kevin's name. After that, we prayed in anticipation of our son's return. Days and weeks passed. We continued to pray with faith, hope, concern, and confidence for Kevin's deliverance from the cult.

During my early years of Christian development, I had heard more mature Christians talk about "praying through." That concept is based in part on Romans 8:16, which says that "the Spirit himself testifies with our spirit that we are God's children." What I understand from that verse is that the Holy Spirit can witness assurance in our hearts about other matters as well.

The night we wrote, "We believe!" in the margin of my Bible, we expressed our assurance that the Holy Spirit had witnessed to our spirits that our prayers would be answered. We continued to pray with growing confidence that God would answer. God had moved us beyond those agonizing "If You can" prayers.

One evening after dinner, I got into our car to run an errand. As I pulled out of the driveway, I saw movement out of the corner of my eye and turned to see my wife waving her arms at me. I stopped the car and rolled down the window. Carolyn called across the street, "Kevin is on the phone and wants to talk with you." I turned off the ignition, raced across the street, hurried into the house, and picked up the phone.

The first words I heard were, "Dad, can I come home?"

"Of course you can!" I responded. "Call back collect in an hour, and I'll tell you which airline desk to go to at the airport. We're so happy you're coming home!"

Kevin flew through the night. The next morning, we gathered him in our arms and took him home—one month to the day from when we had written "We believe!" in our Bible. In a manifestation of God's grace and power, He answered our prayers and flooded our hearts with joy.

WORDS OF WISDOM

The Bible tells us that when God went forth for the salvation of his people, then he "did ride upon his horses and chariots of salvation." And it is the same now. Everything becomes a "chariot of salvation," when God rides upon it . . . he does not command or originate the thing perhaps; but the moment we put it into his hands it becomes his, and he at once turns it into a chariot for us. He makes all things, even bad things, work together for good to all those who trust him. All he needs is to have them entirely committed to him. . . .

Get into your chariot, then. Take each thing that is wrong in your lives as God's chariot for you. No matter who the builder of the wrong may be, whether men or devils, by the time it reaches your side it is God's chariot for you and is meant to carry you to a heavenly place of triumph. Shut out all the second causes and find the Lord in it. Say, "Lord, open my eyes that I may see, not the visible enemy, but your unseen chariots of deliverance."

Hannah Whitall Smith

GOD'S PROMISE

Anything is possible if a person believes.

Mark 9:23 (NL)

PRAYER

O Lord God, in whom we live, and move, and have our being, open our eyes that we may behold thy fatherly presence ever about us.

Draw our hearts to thee with the power of Thy love.

Teach us to be anxious for nothing, and when we have done what thou hast given us to do, help us, O God our Savior, to leave the issue to thy wisdom.

Take from us all doubt and mistrust.

Lift our thoughts up to thee in heaven, and make us to know that all things are possible to us through thy Son our Redeemer. Amen.

Brooke F. Westcott

THE GOD WHO GIVES

Christopher de Vinck

GOD'S WORD

> We can be confident that God will listen to us whenever we ask him for anything in line with his will. And if we know he is listening when we make our requests, we can be sure that he will give us what we ask for.
>
> *1 John 5:14–15 (NL)*

THIS PAST OCTOBER I taught, perhaps, the last class I will ever teach. I have been a teacher for sixteen years, and now I am a school administrator. The new job means a shorter commute and a new challenge. As I looked back to all that I did in the classroom, I became frightened of my new position. How do I start something new all over again? Did I make a mistake in leaving the classroom?

How do you deal with serious decisions you need to make? I share my concerns with my family. I look to people I admire and see what they did with their lives, but then I still have to make the decision on my own.

I have always depended on that deep-inside voice to guide me in my life. That voice didn't fail me when I was hoping to meet my someday wife. That voice didn't fail me when I sought strength as I tried to teach, write, be a husband and father. That voice didn't fail me when I was hoping that my writing would grow.

Someone once said to me that we should ask God for big gifts and graces. We shouldn't be afraid. We aren't greedy people. We know what God likes to hear. We know He likes us to ask for help, and He always helps.

I tell my three children that I cannot solve all their problems, but I can always help them with any difficult situation they encounter along the way.

Change is frightening, but I go home to the same wife, the same children, and to the same cat. They are still there, and I pray to the same God. He's still there, too.

Have you asked God for anything lately? Have you asked Him for something extraordinary? He will not help you win the lottery. He will not help you discover the fountain of youth. You and God both know exactly what things you can ask for. What is the biggest thing missing in your heart? Ask God to help you find that missing part. That deep, personal need is greater than gold. God provides. You just have to ask.

WORDS OF WISDOM

You can talk to God because God listens. Your voice matters in heaven. He takes you very seriously. When you enter his presence, the attendants turn to you to hear your voice. No need to fear that you will be ignored. Even if you stammer or stumble, even if what you have to say impresses no one, it impresses God—and he listens. . . .

Max Lucado

GOD'S PROMISE

My God will meet all your needs according to his glorious riches in Christ Jesus.

Philippians 4:19

PRAYER

Lord, we do not know what we ought to ask of you; you only know what we need; you love us better than we know how to love ourselves. O Father! Give to us, your children, that which we ourselves do not know how to ask. We have no other desire than to accomplish your will. Teach us to pray. Pray yourself in us; for Christ's sake. Amen.

François Fénelon

*W*ords fail to explain how necessary prayer is, and in how many ways the exercise of prayer is profitable. Surely, with good reason the Heavenly Father affirms that the only stronghold of safety is in calling upon his name.

JOHN CALVIN

PRAYER
that
PROTECTS

The righteous face many troubles, but the
LORD rescues them from each and every one.
For the LORD protects them from harm....

Psalm 34:19–20 (NL)

"GOD, PLEASE PROTECT JODY"
Karen Strand

GOD'S WORD

> Jesus said, "Do not let your hearts be troubled. Trust in God; trust also in me."

John 14:1

"PLEASE DON'T DO THIS!" I pleaded with my daughter. On a warm evening in April, we were sitting on the front porch glider when Jody informed me she planned to hitchhike across America . . . alone.

I couldn't believe it. My nineteen−year−old's earlier years had been challenge enough: skipping school, breaking curfews, and experimenting with drugs. Now she had decided a future awaited her in Nashville, singing country and western. Nashville was 3,000 miles from our home in Washington state.

"Honey, if it really means that much to you, we'll buy you a plane ticket. Just don't do such a crazy thing."

Jody tossed her long, honey−colored hair over her shoulder. "Mom, I know you won't understand, but it's more than that. I want to travel, to see the country. And the only way I can afford it is to hit the road."

The morning Jody left, I stood helplessly by, watching her stuff her backpack with personal items and her poetry notebook. I had just handed her a stack of self−addressed, stamped envelopes, when I got an idea. "Jody, would you do me one favor?"

"What's that?" she asked, suspicious.

"Let me videotape you. I want a visual record in case you end up on Unsolved Mysteries."

Her likeness captured on tape, I walked with her to the front porch and gave her a tight hug. "I love you, honey. And I'll be praying for you every day." As she headed down our hill toward the freeway, I watched her figure grow smaller and smaller. My heart broke into smaller pieces yet.

The next day Jody called collect from Oregon. She had gotten a ride with a very nice trucker and would be continuing with him into Idaho. A few days later she called from Utah. I bought a map of the United States and began following her trek with a red marker. Thus began months of following Jody as she made her way south.

In Colorado she spent the night in a rescue mission; in New Mexico her ride ditched her in the middle of the desert. In Texas she learned how to ride the rails. "It's not illegal as long we hop on while the boxcars are moving." Great. Now I had the added worry of her legs getting amputated. She slept in cow pastures, on river banks, and in the superstructure of freeway overpasses. She cooked over open fires with the homeless. Night after night I fell into bed praying, "Oh God, please protect Jody." In my journal I wrote, "For once I've been allowed a trial that is beyond my ability to endure."

Then, one day while driving home from the mall, I turned on the radio to a Christian station just in time to hear a speaker say: "Isn't it odd, that when people are at their wit's end, they often say 'well there's nothing left to do now, but pray.' And yet praying is about the most powerful, the most effective thing we can do."

The words hit hard. Powerful. I'd never thought of my prayers in that way. Instead there had been a lot of begging, filled with pleases: "Please, God, protect Jody. Please, God keep her safe. Please, God, bring her home soon." But power. That was something else.

The next time I prayed for Jody, I began by dwelling on the mightiness and holiness of our God. I told Him how scared I was and how I wasn't going to be able to handle this without Him. I took my map of the United States with the wavy red ink marking Jody's journey and laid it before the Lord. I prayed about who gave her rides, where she spent the night, her health and what she ate, and each person she would come into contact with. I also prayed that she would draw near to God through reading the Bible she had taken along.

It was a turning point for all of my prayers. My daughter was somewhere

on the road. I could not go to her. I could not bring her back. Yet I was not help-less. I could pray! The more I prayed in this new way, the more I understood Philippians 4:6, that if we do not yield to anxiety but make our requests known to God, we will have peace. For me, it meant enough peace to fall blissfully asleep each night.

Jody did make it to Nashville. She sang there, too, although she never made it to stardom. In six months she traveled some 7,000 miles, returning safely home in October. She had a lot of stories to tell, but what she repeated most often was, "Mom, I knew you were praying." She did read her Bible, and she did grow closer to God.

Today, Jody lives in an apartment nearby, has a job, and attends our church. I no longer rush before God when I'm in trouble, praying "please" this and "please" that. I take time to worship Him, tell Him all the details, and acknowledge His sovereignty.

And I keep thanking Him for the day I learned how to pray.

WORDS OF WISDOM

Think of the things you do not worry about. Perhaps you never worry about whether you will be able to get water out of the faucet in your kitchen, or maybe you do not worry about a tree falling on your house.

Now ask yourself why you do not worry about such things. Is it because, in the case of running water, that it has always been there every time you wanted it, or that a tree has never fallen on your house before? Certainty breeds trust, doesn't it?

We can be just as certain and just as worry-free about God's love, protection, and provision because he has never gone back on a single one of his promises.

Billy Graham

GOD'S PROMISE

Don't worry about anything; instead, pray about everything. Tell God what you need, and thank him for all he has done. If you do this, you will experience God's peace, which is far more wonderful than the human mind can understand. His peace will guard your hearts and minds as you live in Christ Jesus.

Philippians 4: 6–7 (NL)

PRAYER

Ere thou sleepest, gently lay
Every troubled thought away.
Put off worry and distress
As thou puttest off thy dress.
Drop thy worry and thy care
In the quiet arms of prayer.

Lord, thou knowest how I live;
All I've done amiss, forgive;
All the good I've tried to do
Hallow, bless, and carry through.
All I love in safety keep,
While, in thee, I fall asleep.

Source unknown

COLLISION
Ed Hilton, as told to Quin Sherrer

GOD'S WORD

> Be not far from me, O God;
>   come quickly, O my God, to help me.
>
>   *Psalm 71:12*

HOW CLOSE I CAME TO DEATH! I could have been knocked unconscious or trapped in the cab to die that fateful spring afternoon, leaving my two beautiful children without a father and my wife a widow.

On March 19, 1996, about five o'clock in the afternoon, I was making a routine delivery for the courier company I worked for. In the back of my truck was ten thousand pounds of paper—six full skids of computer paper. I was traveling north on 75 Central in Dallas. The highway is four lanes wide, and I was in the second to right lane. The traffic was moderate.

All of a sudden I heard brakes squealing and saw a fast-moving car cutting across the lanes, hitting my truck and causing me to lose control. My vehicle rammed through a guard rail, taking down a steel lamp post as it went. Then I realized the truck was going off the side of some sort of bridge. I remember calling out, "Lord, help me!"

The truck rolled and landed upside down on an entrance ramp, about ten feet below, then slid several feet. The cab area was crushed, the windshield was blown out, and hot oil was pouring into the cab from the engine.

As soon as I shut off the ignition, I saw something was on fire, The next thing I knew—just seconds, it seemed—the truck burst into flames. "Jesus, please help me get out," I screamed. Managing to unbuckle my seat belt, I scrambled out through the smashed windshield.

The medical team at the hospital could not believe I was not seriously hurt. I had some cuts, singed hair, and a couple of minor burns. The doctor said I was lucky. But luck did not save me; God's hand of protection saved me.

After two hours of examinations and treatment, I was released.

Later when I saw the truck, I could not believe the wreckage; it was smashed almost flat.

Afterward this Scripture came to me: "When you walk through the fire, you will not be burned; the flames will not set you ablaze. For I am the LORD, your God, the Holy One of Israel, your Savior" (Isaiah 43:2–3).

I have thought a lot about how close I came to being killed, as certainly would have happened had I not gotten out of the truck before it exploded! If the seat belt had not unsnapped, if the windshield had not been smashed open. . . . I thank God that I'm alive, and I am determined to fulfill God's will for my life.

WORDS OF WISDOM:
THE HAPPINESS OF BEING ALIVE

Once life has almost been
taken from you,
When for some strange reason you emerge
    from death
and blink
with new eyes upon the old
almost forgotten universe,
then you can understand once more
the value of sea and stars,
of happiness uncontainable,
the sheer relief and delight of being alive
that turns your eyes repeatedly
upwards
with thanksgiving
then straight outward
declaring peace over and over again
to those who with heads bent low
see mud not stars.

Kathy Keay

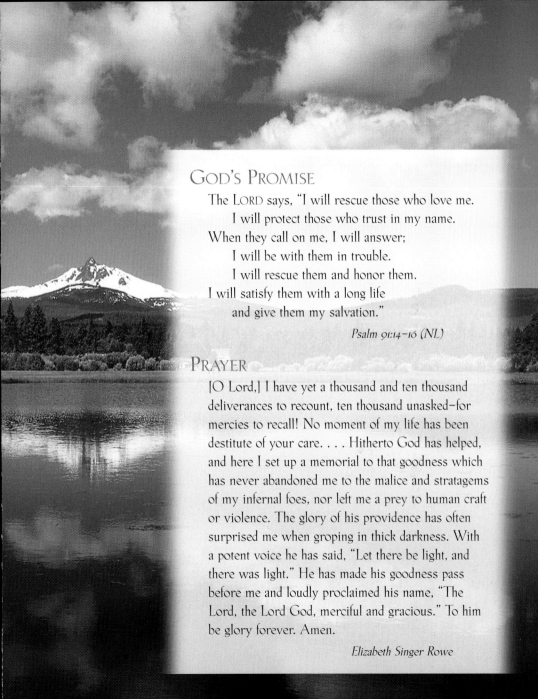

GOD'S PROMISE

The LORD says, "I will rescue those who love me.
   I will protect those who trust in my name.
When they call on me, I will answer;
   I will be with them in trouble.
   I will rescue them and honor them.
I will satisfy them with a long life
   and give them my salvation."

Psalm 91:14–16 (NL)

PRAYER

[O Lord,] I have yet a thousand and ten thousand
deliverances to recount, ten thousand unasked-for
mercies to recall! No moment of my life has been
destitute of your care. . . . Hitherto God has helped,
and here I set up a memorial to that goodness which
has never abandoned me to the malice and stratagems
of my infernal foes, nor left me a prey to human craft
or violence. The glory of his providence has often
surprised me when groping in thick darkness. With
a potent voice he has said, "Let there be light, and
there was light." He has made his goodness pass
before me and loudly proclaimed his name, "The
Lord, the Lord God, merciful and gracious." To him
be glory forever. Amen.

Elizabeth Singer Rowe

GROWING ROOTS
Philip Gulley

GOD'S WORD

> I pray that from his glorious, unlimited resources he will give you
> mighty inner strength through his Holy Spirit. And I pray that
> Christ will be more and more at home in your hearts as you trust
> in him. May your roots go down deep into the soil of God's
> marvelous love.
>
> *Ephesians 3:16–17 (NL)*

HAD AN OLD NEIGHBOR when I was growing up named Doctor
Gibbs. He didn't look like any doctor I'd ever known. Every time I saw
him, he we wearing denim overalls and a straw hat, the front brim of
which was green sunglass plastic. He smiled a lot, a smile that matched
his hat—old and crinkly and well-worn. He never yelled at us for
playing in his yard. I remember him as someone who was a lot nicer
than circumstances warranted.

When Doctor Gibbs wasn't saving lives, he was planting trees. His
house sat on ten acres, and his life-goal was to make it a forest. The
good doctor had some interesting theories concerning plant husbandry.
He came from the "No pain, no gain" school of horticulture. He never
watered his new trees, which flew in the face of conventional wisdom.
Once I asked why. He said that watering plants spoiled them, and that if
you water them, each successive tree generation will grow weaker and
weaker. So you have to make things rough for them and weed out the
weenie trees early on.

He talked about how watering trees made for shallow roots, and how
trees that weren't watered had to grow deep roots in search of moisture.
I took him to mean that deep roots were to be treasured.

So he never watered his trees. He'd plant an oak and, instead of
watering it every morning he'd beat it with a rolled up newspaper.

Smack! Slap! Pow! I asked him why he did that, and he said it was to get the tree's attention.

Doctor Gibbs went to glory a couple years after I left home. Every now and again, I walk by his house and look at the trees that I'd watched him plant some twenty-five years ago. They're granite strong now. Big and robust. Those trees wake up in the morning and beat their chests and drink their coffee black.

I planted a couple trees a few years back. Carried water to them for a solid summer. Sprayed them. Prayed over them. The whole nine yards. Two years of coddling has resulted in trees that expect to be waited on hand and foot. Whenever a cold wind blows in, they tremble and chatter their branches. Sissy trees.

Funny thing about those trees of Doctor Gibbs. Adversity and deprivation seemed to benefit them in ways comfort and ease never could.

Every night before I go to bed, I go check on my two sons. I stand over them and watch their little bodies, the rising and falling of life within. I often pray for them. Mostly I pray that their lives will be easy. "Lord, spare them from hardship." But lately I've been thinking that it's time to change my prayer.

Has to do with the inevitability of cold winds that hit us at the core. I know my children are going to encounter hardship, and my praying they won't is naïve. There's always a cold wind blowing somewhere.

So I'm changing my eventide prayer. Because life is tough, whether we want it to be or not. Instead, I'm going to pray that my sons' roots grow deep, so they can draw strength from the hidden sources of the eternal God.

Too many times we pray for ease, but that's a prayer seldom met. What we need to do is pray for roots that reach deep into the Eternal, so when the rains fall and the winds blow, we won't be swept asunder.

WORDS OF WISDOM

None of us knows what lies ahead for our children. . . . Finding direction in life isn't a do-it-yourself task. Our children are being guided. As they seek God, his plan will unfold in their lives. We can look forward to their future with confidence and certainty that they are safe under God's protective wing.

Pam Vredevelt

GOD'S PROMISE

So do not fear, for I am with you;
    Do not be dismayed, for I am your God.
I will strengthen you and help you;
    I will uphold you with my righteous right hand.

Isaiah 41:10

PRAYER

Father, hear us, we are praying,
Hear the words our hearts are
    saying,
We are praying for our children.

Keep them from the powers of evil,
From the secret, hidden peril,
Father, hear us for our children.

From the whirlpool that would
    suck them
From the treacherous quicksand,
    pluck them,
Father, hear us for our children.

From the worldling's hollow gladness,
From the sting of faithless sadness,
Father, Father, keep our children.

Through life's troubled waters steer
    them,
Through life's bitter battle cheer them
Father, Father, be Thou near them.

Amy Carmichael

THE LATE COMMUTE
Mary Lou Carney

GOD'S WORD

> Are not all angels ministering spirits sent to serve those who will inherit salvation?
>
> *Hebrews 1:14*

LIKE ANY MOTHER, I had always worried about my daughter's safety. But after Amy Jo's divorce, I seemed to worry even more. How vulnerable she seemed—especially when she elected to take a class that meant she would have a late train ride home from Chicago two nights a week.

I was especially worried about her getting safely to the train station. Her class was held in an area many blocks from the station, and I shivered to think of my petite, blond girl walking alone on the dark city streets.

I was driving home from Bible school on one of Amy Jo's class nights, trying not to think about all the things that could happen, when I seemed to hear a voice commanding: Pray for a guardian angel! I knew it was God encouraging me to trust Him, so I did.

"Please, God, send a guardian angel to walk to the train station with Amy Jo tonight."

I felt a deep peace as I turned into my driveway.

Next morning, I couldn't wait to talk to Amy Jo.

"Any trouble getting to the train station?" were the first words out of my mouth when she came downstairs for breakfast.

She broke into a wide smile.

"Nope! I had a guardian angel!"

Amy Jo went on to describe how, on impulse, she'd paused at the door of the classroom and asked if anyone might be planning to catch a train.

"Yo, that would be me!" one of the biggest men in the class said. And he walked with Amy Jo all the way to the door of her train.

WORDS OF WISDOM

"What a Friend we have in Jesus!" His hand
keeps us, not only when we go through the
valley of the shadow of death but also before
that. When we pray, "Take my hand, Lord,
and hold me tight," the Lord does it. . . .

My father used to say to us, when we
were children and had to go away from home
for a while, "Children, don't forget, when
Jesus takes your hand, then he holds you
tight. And when Jesus keeps you tight, he
guides you through life. And when Jesus
guides you through life, one day he brings
you safely home."

Corrie ten Boom

GOD'S PROMISE

If you make the LORD your refuge,
    if you make the Most High your shelter,
no evil will conquer you;
    no plague will come near your dwelling.
For he orders his angels
    to protect you wherever you go.

Psalm 91:9–11 (NL)

Prayer

May the strength of God pilot us.
May the power of God preserve us.
May the wisdom of God instruct us.
May the hand of God protect us.
May the way of God direct us.
May the shield of God defend us.

May the host of God guard us
against the snares of the Evil One
and the temptations of the world.

May Christ be with us.
Christ before us.
Christ in us.
Christ over us.

May Thy salvation, O Lord,
be always ours this day and evermore.
Amen.

St. Patrick

*M*any people tend to associate prayer with separation from others, but real prayer brings us closer to our fellow human beings. Prayer is the first and indispensable discipline of compassion precisely because prayer is also the first expression of human solidarity. Why is this so? Because the Spirit who prays in us is the Spirit by whom all human beings are brought together in unity and community.

HENRI J.M. NOUWEN

PRAYER
that
CARES *for*
OTHERS

I urge you, first of all, pray for all people.
As you make your requests, plead for
God's mercy upon them, and give thanks.

1 Timothy 2:1 (NL)

FRIENDSHIP
Mike Mason

GOD'S WORD

No one has ever seen God. But if we love each other, God lives in us, and his love is made complete in us.

1 John 4:12

YEARS AGO I OPENED a fortune cookie and read, "You will have many friends." As I had no friends at the time (or at least felt I had none), this struck me as a promise from God. I put this tiny piece of paper into my wallet and carried it around until the day it came true. Then I passed it on to a friend who needed it.

I still remember the day I realized that this promise had been fulfilled in my life. It happened in the twinkling of an eye. One day I had no friends, and the next day I had more friends than I could easily count. Something amazing happened to me. What was it?

Although I had been a Christian for many years, when I say I had no friends, I mean that seriously. As a writer, an introvert, a contemplative, I had limited time for people. Yes, there was my family. I had a good marriage and a daughter I loved, but beyond this small circle my relationships were shallow. I do not mean that my conversations never got beyond the weather. No, I had many meaningful interactions with people. But at some deep level that I tried to ignore, I did not feel connected. I had many contacts, but no real community.

Even if I did connect with someone, the moment that person was out of sight I would break the connection. Something in me broke it, as if somehow I had learned that it was not safe to get too close to people. I could have moved to the other side of the world without a twinge of regret.

If I were to retrace all the steps in the process through which I emerged from this prison, I would have to write another book. Yet in a sense, the change I experienced was simple and did happen overnight. If a traveler wants to get to New York and suddenly realizes he is heading in the wrong direction, all he has to do is turn around. He has not yet arrived at New York. He may still have a long journey ahead. But at least now he is not lost. He knows he is headed in the right direction, and this makes all the difference.

One incident marks the moment when I changed direction. It happened on my birthday, when my wife had invited some "friends" over for cake. Usually I like to spend my birthday quietly, but for once I grudgingly consented to a small party. Predictably I was out of sorts, in no mood to put on a happy face for company. Somehow I faked my way through a painful evening.

Toward the end, as we sat around in the living room, someone suggested that they pray for me. Bowing my head, I listened with a mixture of skepticism and vague hope to some very nice, very ordinary prayers for my well-being. As usual something inside me was already preparing to break any connection that might be formed with these people.

The prayer time came to an end, and nothing happened. At least, I thought nothing had happened until I opened my eyes. Then, looking around that small circle of familiar faces, all at once they appeared strangely bright, luminously tender and present. For reasons I could not fathom, tears came to my eyes.

For some time there was silence. All eyes were upon me.

"What's going on?" asked my wife eventually. "What are you feeling?"

Still for some time I struggled in silence with my emotions.

Finally I took a deep breath and said, "I'm feeling that everyone here loves me."

Like a pebble cast into the ocean, this was a seemingly small event, yet its ripples turned into waves, and those waves are still rocking my foundations in a way that feels as gentle and wonderful as the rocking of a cradle.

John wrote, "This is love: not that we loved God, but that he loved us" (1 John 4:10). Whether with God or with people, receiving love is the key to friendship. For as I am loved, so shall I love.

It is one thing to believe that God loves me. But to believe that people love me too, and to receive their love as from God—in some ways this has come to me as an even greater revelation. As George MacDonald wrote to his wife, "Thank you for your precious love—the most precious thing I have: for I will not divide between the love of God directly to me and that which flows through you."

WORDS OF WISDOM

One day a friend of mine was walking through a shopping mall with his two-year-old son. The child was in a particularly cantankerous mood, fussing and fuming. The frustrated father tried everything to quiet his son, but nothing seemed to help. The child simply would not obey. Then, under some special inspiration, the father scooped up his son and, holding him close to his chest, began singing an impromptu love song. None of the words rhymed. He sang off key. And yet, as best he could, this father began sharing his heart. "I love you," he sang. "I'm so glad you're my boy. You make me happy. I like the way you laugh." On they went from one store to the next. Quietly the father continued singing off key and making up words that did not rhyme. The child relaxed and became still, listening to this strange and wonderful song. Finally, they finished shopping and went to the car. As the father opened the door and prepared to buckle his son into the carseat, the child lifted his head and said simply, "Sing it to me again, Daddy! Sing it to me again!"

Prayer is a little like that. With simplicity of heart we allow ourselves to be gathered up into the arms of the Father and let him sing his love song over us.

Richard J. Foster

GOD'S PROMISE

I am convinced that nothing can ever separate us from his love. Death can't, and life can't. The angels can't, and the demons can't. Our fears for today, our worries about tomorrow, and even the powers of hell can't keep God's love away. Whether we are high above the sky or in the deepest ocean, nothing in all creation will ever be able to separate us from the love of God that is revealed in Christ Jesus our Lord.

Romans 8:38–39 (NL)

PRAYER

Jesus, how sweet is the very thought of you! You fill my heart with joy. The
sweetness of your love surpasses the sweetness of honey. Nothing sweeter
than you can be described; no words can express the joy of your love. Only
those who have tasted your love for themselves can comprehend it. In your
love you listen to all my prayers, even when my wishes are childish, my
words confused, and my thoughts foolish. And you answer my prayers, not
according to my own misdirected desires, which would bring only bitter
misery; but according to my real needs, which brings me sweet joy. Thank
you, Jesus, for giving yourself to me.

Bernard of Clairvaux

COMFORT ONE ANOTHER

Phyllis Hobe

GOD'S WORD

> Encourage one another and build each other up, just as in fact you are doing.
>
> *1 Thessalonians 5:11*

WHEN MY MARRIAGE was ending some years ago, it was a difficult time for me. I was looking for a new place to live and rebuild my life, and I was short of money. Exhausted from disappointment, fear and hurt, I would cry unexpectedly, no matter where I was, so I tried not to see anyone because I thought people might think I was looking for pity. But when my friend Lillian called and said, "Come and have lunch with me," I couldn't say no. I needed her warmth and love more than ever. Still, I was determined not to cry because Lillian had enough pain of her own and I didn't want to inflict any of mine. For years she had suffered from arthritis, and every move was an agony.

I felt guilty sitting in Lillian's kitchen, letting her make our favorite BLTs. "Let me do something," I said, "You shouldn't be waiting on me."

"No, no," she said, "it's good for me to move around."

I literally basked in her care as we lingered at the table, each with our own pain. Lillian talked freely about hers, but I didn't mention mine.

Before I left, Lillian asked me to pray with her, which we often did together. I welcomed the opportunity to ask God's blessing for my dear friend, but before I could offer a word in her behalf, Lillian began to pray out loud for me.

"My friend has a broken heart, Lord," she said, "and her pain is as real as mine. Help her as You are surely helping me. Ease the pain, take away her fear and share her tears."

I couldn't speak because I was crying, but for the first time my tears brought me comfort. Somehow, because my friend was with me, I felt as if Christ Himself was there, lifting my pain from me.

By keeping my hurt to myself, I had prevented Christ from ministering to me. So now, when I have more tears than I can handle, I pray for a friend to share them.

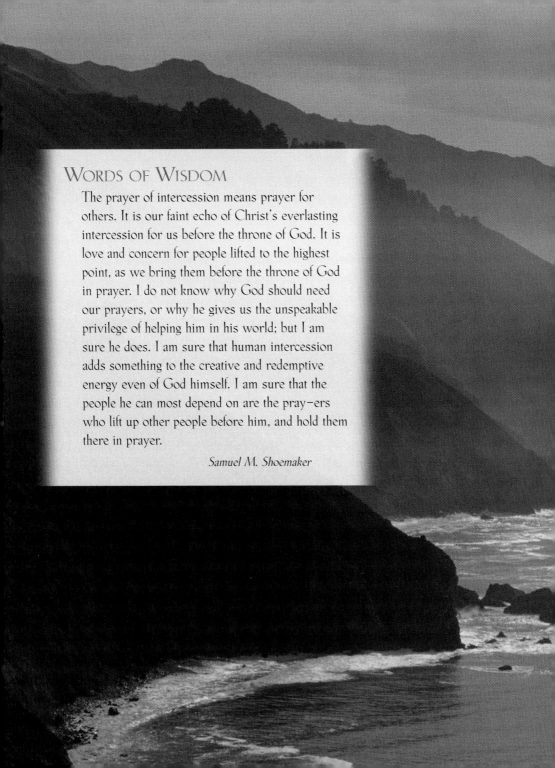

WORDS OF WISDOM

The prayer of intercession means prayer for others. It is our faint echo of Christ's everlasting intercession for us before the throne of God. It is love and concern for people lifted to the highest point, as we bring them before the throne of God in prayer. I do not know why God should need our prayers, or why he gives us the unspeakable privilege of helping him in his world; but I am sure he does. I am sure that human intercession adds something to the creative and redemptive energy even of God himself. I am sure that the people he can most depend on are the pray-ers who lift up other people before him, and hold them there in prayer.

Samuel M. Shoemaker

GOD'S PROMISE

Jesus said, "If two of you on earth agree about anything you ask for, it will be done for you by my Father in heaven. For where two or three come together in my name, there am I with them."

Matthew 18:19–20

PRAYER

Christ,
praying in the Garden while others slept
you know the necessity
and the pain
of standing alone.
Be with me now in my loneliness.
Help me to find strength in solitariness,
peace in the silence,
and the presence of God in the absence of friends.
Turn my thoughts from myself
that I may seek
not so much to find companionship
as to give companionship to others.

Margaret T. Taylor

THE BEST GIFT

Leslie Parrott, as told to Jane Johnson Struck

GOD'S WORD

Dear brothers and sisters, pray for us.

1 Thessalonians 5:25 (NL)

WHEN MY HUSBAND, Les, and I discovered I was pregnant with our son, John, we were delighted! But thirteen weeks into my pregnancy, complications started and never stopped.

I went to the doctor, who ordered an ultrasound. She uncovered a uterine condition that put me at high risk for a second trimester miscarriage. Subsequent ultrasounds showed a one-in-a-million problem with the placenta that limited John's growth. Every time we went to the doctor, the news was worse. We dreaded each visit.

By week eighteen, I developed pregnancy-induced hypertension and was put on complete bed rest. I was given steroids to help John's lungs develop; the doctors knew that with his tiny size, if John couldn't make it to week twenty-eight, he wouldn't survive. I felt miserable all over, and the medications made it worse. I was even too sick for visitors. That's why the prayers of others were so important to me.

Every time the doctors expressed a concern about John's lack of growth, friends and family started praying. There were times we hadn't even had an opportunity to mention we were going to the doctor, and someone would call to say, "I was up praying for you all last night. Just wanted you to know." People who didn't even know us prayed faithfully for us! I've never known that kind of support before.

Miraculously, we made it to week twenty-eight. On February 8, 1998, John was born. He weighed one pound, eight ounces. He immediately dropped to one pound because of a problem with his intestines. John had to have major surgery, then was on total life support and a ventilator.

We were tender emotionally. I was recovering from surgery, and John was so

tiny, Les's wedding band fit all the way up to his little shoulders. But the prayer support of people who gathered around us kept us going. I felt a strength, a peace beyond myself that enabled me to get through everything we faced.

After three months, John came home. He was still on oxygen and weighed three pounds—the smallest baby the hospital has ever released.

Today, John's such a little go-getter. By his first birthday, he weighed fourteen pounds, five ounces. When you have a preemie, there's no guarantee about his physical or developmental well-being. That's helped me focus on what's really important: John's knowledge of God.

Our experience has changed my view of prayer. The best gifts we were given were those prayers for baby John; no other gift has meant so much. I now know with new certainty it's the most powerful way I can join others in their struggles, too.

WORDS OF WISDOM

I believe the greatest cry around the world today is "Pray for me." All of us are here today because someone has prayed for us. I know I am indebted to so many people for their wonderful prayers. Martin Luther said that the shoemaker makes shoes, the tailor makes clothes, and the Christian prays. Prayer can change a person's life; it can change the world. Prayer is a challenge to me. If I pray for someone, it challenges me to love and to help that person.

James H. Davis

GOD'S PROMISE

The earnest prayer of a righteous person has great power and wonderful results.

James 5:16 (NL)

PRAYER

Father, it's your love that heals us, body and soul. Thank you for the way you reveal this tremendous love through other people. Help me to realize that persistent prayer is nothing other than persistent love. May I remember this when I am tempted to quit praying. As I persist, reveal your love through me. Amen.

Ann Spangler

POST–OP
Mike Nappa

GOD'S WORD

Paul went in to see [Publius' father] and, after prayer, placed his hands on him and healed him.

Acts 28:8

SOMETHING WAS TRYING to kill me. I could feel it in my gut.

This was supposed to be a simple operation. Though only thirty–three years old, my gall bladder had become so diseased it resembled an old man's and was causing me great pain, making it impossible for me to eat. The surgeon recommended the standard treatment: remove the gallbladder.

I agreed, eager to be rid of the malfunctioning organ. Two days after Christmas in 1996, I entered the hospital for a routine surgery. The anesthesiologist administered the anesthesia, and I was soon ushered into a dark and dreamless sleep.

Ouch! Something was wrong. I couldn't open my eyes or move a muscle, but I could feel someone tearing inside my stomach. The pain was unbearable, but I couldn't scream. Had I awakened before the surgery was over? I managed a weak thought. Help me, Lord. . . . Moments later I welcomed the darkness that swirled back into my consciousness.

The next time I awoke I knew the surgery was over because I opened my eyes and saw myself in the recovery room. The pain in my stomach, where the surgery had been performed, was overwhelming. I groaned and immediately tried to sit up, not caring that the two nurses near me were trying to hold me down. This isn't supposed to hurt this much! I thought. Something is wrong.

Apparently I was too strong for my two helpers. The nurse in charge quickly sent the other running to get help to hold me down. I was dangerously close to ripping the IV out of my arm and could possibly tear the fresh stitches in my stomach.

I knew I needed to relax, ignore the pain, and lie back down, but I wasn't strong enough to do it myself. I grabbed on to the metal bar of my bed and became aware of the one nurse left behind still trying to calm me down.

"Pray for me," I croaked to her. Then I demanded it. "Somebody pray for me!"

"Okay, okay, just lie—"

"Pray for me!"

"Okay." She took a deep breath and placed her hand on my arm. "Heavenly Father . . ."

As soon as she spoke that name, a sense of peace flooded through me, starting at my head and trickling all the way down to my toes. I felt the Holy Spirit saying, "I'm here. No matter what happens, I'm here."

I watched my hand relax its grip on the bar. I still felt pain, but I was in control of my body once more. Slowly, I lay back onto the gurney. The nurse kept praying. To be honest, I don't know what she said, but I watched her lips move as she continued praying for me.

"Read to me," I said. "From the Bible. Read to me." More medical staff arrived and were beginning to surround me.

"Get me a Bible," the nurse commanded. I saw someone pass a book into her open hand. She flipped it open, paging through to find what she wanted. Then she began to read, "'The LORD is my shepherd, I shall not want . . .'"

I closed my eyes. The merciful darkness soon came swirling back into my mind. *Thank you, Lord,* I whispered to myself. Then I slept.

When I woke again later, all was calm. I was sore and weak, but the agonizing pain had been dulled by pain medication. I was in a private room, now. My wife sat next to me, pale-faced.

"You had a rough time in there," she said. "I was really afraid for you."

So was I, I thought. *So was I.*

My operation had had complications. While removing my gallbladder, the surgeon had accidentally spilled scores of gallstones inside my body. He had carefully removed each stone, but that added task had apparently triggered unexpected pain for me.

I am grateful for that nurse—a woman who, at my point of great need, was willing to pray for me—and for my Father, who paused to answer her prayer.

WORDS OF WISDOM

The real business of your life as a saved soul is intercessory prayer.

Oswald Chambers

GOD'S PROMISE

The prayer offered in faith will heal the sick, and the Lord will make them well.

James 5:15 (NL)

PRAYER

This morning, O Christ, bird songs pour in through the open windows of hospitals. There are pain-glazed eyes looking out to where trees—dressed in the green lace of spring—are eloquent of recurring life.

Thou, O Christ, art the author of this new life. Wilt thou even now visit the sick as thou were ever wont to do? Lay upon fevered brows the cool fingers of thy love. May those who suffer, whom we name now before thee, feel thy presence at their bedsides, and have the realization at this moment of thy touch, bringing to them new life and strength and health.

We thank thee for the healings that have come, for the restorations that have been received, for many prayers answered. We thank thee that thou dost still heal today. We thank thee for this, the sweetest word of the gospel message, that thou dost come with healing in thy wings.

We thank thee that thou has heard and answered this prayer, born of our faith in thee as the Great Physician. In thy name, we pray. Amen.

Peter Marshall

$\mathcal{A}$t the center of our being we are hushed. The experience is more profound than mere silence or lack of words. There is stillness, to be sure, but it is a listening stillness. We feel more alive, more active, than we ever do when our minds are askew with muchness and manyness. Something deep inside us has been awakened and brought to attention. Our spirit is on tiptoe—alert and listening.

RICHARD J. FOSTER

Section Four

PRAYER
that
LISTENS

Listen to me! For I have excellent things to tell you.

Proverbs 8:6 (NL)

A Prompting from the Spirit

Joni Eareckson Tada

God's Word

> Today, if you hear God's voice,
> do not harden your hearts. . . .
>
> *Psalm 95:7–8*

RUSH FROM WORK. Meet Judy at Hamburger Hamlet. Glance at menu. Scarf down Chicken Caesar. Pay bill, exit restaurant, put down lift and wheel into van. Oh yes, stop and pray with Judy before heading in different directions. After our "Amens," she headed for her car. While I waited for my van to warm up, I breathed deeply, trying to slow down my heart from the fast-paced day. It was evening now, a different pace. And I was heading to my church to speak to our women's group.

As I pulled out of the parking space, I noticed a woman wearing a baseball cap leaving the restaurant. *I wonder who she is? That baseball cap . . . her scraggly hair.* Suddenly, I sensed a powerful urge to ask her to come to my church to hear me speak. *Yes, she must come . . . she should come to hear me. She needs to hear what I have to say.*

"This is ridiculous," I said out loud, alone in my van. Cars were backing up behind me. Should I follow through on the impulse? "What am I supposed to do, God? Roll down my window, yell to her to come over here and say, 'Hey, I think you ought to follow me to church!' This is silly!" I honked at Judy. She jumped out of her car, ran over to my window, and I told her about the strange prompting. Judy glanced at the woman on the sidewalk, and then at the line of waiting cars. "You're blocking traffic, Joni, you'll be late for your meeting."

All the way to church I berated myself for not inviting the woman with the baseball cap to come to church. "Lord," I prayed out loud, "next time I won't flinch. I'll follow through. I promise I'll listen to your promptings!" Ten minutes later, as I was pulling into the church parking lot, I was surprised to see Judy arrive right behind me. "You're not going to believe what happened," she said, as I saw another van park right next to her.

Apparently, after I left the Hamburger Hamlet, the woman in the baseball cap approached Judy and asked who I was. This was too weird for my friend.

"Joni almost invited you to come hear her speak," she said. "Would you like to go? I'll show you the way."

There in the church parking lot I heard her story. "Earlier, my husband and I were at the UCLA cancer clinic, and we stopped to eat on our way home." Her voice cracked; her husband squeezed her shoulder. Joyce—that was her name—continued: "I've had breast cancer for four years, and two hours ago I learned that the cancer is now in my brain. It's inoperable. You looked so . . . happy. I don't know what to do, where to turn. And so, we're here."

My mouth dropped open. I now understood the scraggly hair under the baseball cap—chemotherapy. I also understood why the Holy Spirit had urged me to halt in the middle of everything and invite her, a complete stranger, to come hear me speak.

That night, as Joyce and her husband sat in the front row, I talked about heaven and hope, grace and the gospel of Christ. The two strangers had an opportunity to bow their heads and pray to open up their hearts to Jesus. I shudder to think the opportunity was almost lost. It was almost lost because I let awkwardness override it . . . I let embarrassment dissuade me . . . I pooh-poohed it, thinking, She's a stranger, for goodness sake.

Yes, for goodness sake, I wonder how many of us sense an urge to reach out, but then do nothing—we second-guess the prompting and ignore the Spirit's leading. I learned that night that every urge to do good, every prompting to share the gospel is a prompting from God. We need not second-guess. God's Word through Paul in 2 Corinthians 6:2 pushes us into action: "I tell you, now is the time of God's favor, now is the day of salvation."

This week you'll hear God's still, small voice whisper, "Say something to her . . . Invite him to . . . Make that call . . . Forgive him of . . . Apologize for . . . Check on her. . . ." You may be tempted to brush it off, but don't.

Seize the moment. Now is the time of God's favor. This is the day of salvation.

The prompting may never pass your way again. And neither might that person. Forever.

WORDS OF WISDOM

A spiritual life requires discipline because we need to learn to listen to God, who constantly speaks but whom we seldom hear. When, however, we learn to listen, our lives become obedient lives. The word "obedient" comes from the Latin word audire, which means "listening.". . . Jesus' life was a life of obedience. He was always listening to the Father, always attentive to his voice, always alert for his directions. Jesus was "all ear." That is true prayer: being all ear for God. The core of all prayer is indeed listening, obediently standing in the presence of God.

Henri J.M. Nouwen

GOD'S PROMISE

As for God, his way is perfect; the word of the LORD is flawless.

Psalm 18:30

PRAYER

Father,
Let my existence be ruled by a great silence.
Let my soul be listening, be given to the needs of others.
Let me be silent in my innermost being, not asserting myself.
Let my soul be detached, not grasping at anything in this world.
And thus overcome in my life the power of habit, daily routine, dullness, fatigue
    and fear.
Let me create within myself a carefree tranquility, a place for every encounter,
    unreserved receptivity, and unhurried disposition.
Extinguish within me the feelings of self-importance and the last stirrings of
    my ego,
And make me gentle.
Let me answer thoughts and situations rather than words.
Through Jesus Christ our Lord,
who taught us to be holy as you are holy. Amen.

Hassan Dehqani-Tafti, one-time Bishop in Iran, now in exile

ARE YOU LISTENING?

Lani Carroll Hinkle

GOD'S WORD

> I have stilled and quieted my soul;
>> Like a weaned child with its mother,
>> Like a weaned child is my soul within me.

Psalm 131:2

I REMEMBER THE FIRST TIME I heard God speak to me clearly. I had just had a miscarriage after three years of infertility. Nothing was making sense to me, I was sad, and I felt alone. Unable to sleep in the middle of the night, I wrapped myself in a quilt and went into what was supposed to be the baby's room to pray. There in the dark, I found myself unable to do anything but ask God to let me know he was with me. And there, for the first time, I heard God's "still small" voice: "I'm here. You're going to be all right."

An incredible sense of peace settled over me as I realized that I'd really heard God! It was so clear that, at that moment, it didn't matter so much whether I would have a baby or not. What mattered was that God had told me that I would be all right because He was with me.

The next morning, however, I began to wonder why God chose that moment to speak to me. For nearly three years, my husband and I had been praying, as had friends and church members. We'd prayed for direction, faith, a baby. We'd read the story of Hannah and Samuel a million times. Why hadn't we heard him clearly through all of that?

Looking back, I realize that I hadn't been quiet enough to hear. I heard that night because I was completely still. It was quiet, it was dark, and I came to God with no agenda except to find him. My prayers before that time had been full of activity: asking him, telling him, reminding him of Scripture.

Silence is a critical part of listening prayer. Most of the time, whether we're caught up in the activity of ministry or even the fervency of prayer, we find it much easier to talk. In this day and age, in this culture, we've lost the art—and

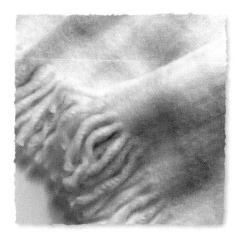

the discipline—of simply being silent in God's presence and waiting expectantly to hear His voice.

We know how to talk to God, but we struggle with listening—for a variety of reasons. As in any loving relationship, however, two-way communication with God is crucial. He is, after all, a relational God, and he delights in speaking with as well as listening to his children. His voice is so important in our lives, whether it is convicting us, ministering to us, directing us, or refreshing us.

Simply put, he speaks. Are you listening?

WORDS OF WISDOM

During our prayer times we have the opportunity to listen.
We listen for the still, small voice of God speaking to our
souls. We listen for the experience of love that he brings to us.
We are uplifted by his Presence entering into our hearts,
enriching and inspiring us to go out and walk upon higher and
more loving pathways. Through prayer, he leads us to step
above the stumbling blocks which have tripped us in the past.
He leads us to accept responsibilities and to face challenges
that we never would have faced before. He leads us to dream
dreams and to filter them through his prayer screen of divine
approval. Then he helps his plans for us to find their spiritual
fulfillment. . . . It is a way to let God fulfill his desires for us.

David C. Cook III

GOD'S PROMISE

In repentance and rest is your salvation,
in quietness and trust is your strength. . . .

Isaiah 30:15

PRAYER

Lord, teach me to pray.
It sounds exciting, put like that.
It sounds real. An exploration.
A chance to do more than catalogue
and list the things I want,
to an eternal Father Christmas.
The chance of meeting you,
of drawing closer to the love that made me
and keeps me, and knows me.
And, Lord, it's only just begun.
There is so much more of you,

of love, the limitless expanse of knowing you.
I could be frightened, Lord, in this wide country.
It could be lonely, but you are here, with me.

The chance of learning about myself,
of facing up to what I am.
Admitting my resentments,
bringing my anger to you, my disappointments, my frustration.
And finding that when I do,
when I stop struggling and shouting
and let go
you are still there.
Still loving.

Sometimes, Lord, often—
I don't know what to say to you.
But I still come, in quiet
for the comfort of two friends
sitting in silence.
And it's then, Lord, that I learn most from you.
When my mind slows down,
and my heart stops racing.
When I let go and wait in the quiet,
realizing that all the things I was going to ask for
you know already.
Then, Lord, without words,
in the stillness
you are there . . .
And I love you.
Lord, teach me to pray.

Eddie Askew

VISITING THE SNEADS

Charlotte Adelsperger

GOD'S WORD

> Anyone who is willing to hear should listen and understand!
> And be sure to pay attention to what you hear.
>
> *Mark 4:23–24 (NL)*

HAVE YOU EVER HAD the sense of being pulled in many different directions by all there is to do? An experience I had as a young mother taught me to allow prayer to prioritize my tasks.

I was pregnant and tired. Most of my energy was going into caring for our toddler, Karen. But one day, with snow falling outside and a whirlwind of errands swirling in my head, a particular "to-do" item came to mind.

It was early as I began my cherished quiet time. I prayed silently and read my Bible. After a time, I took out a notebook and listed the many things I "needed" to do. Sensing God's presence, I felt a loving desire to put Mr. and Mrs. Snead, homebound members of our church, at the top of my list.

I knew making time to visit them wouldn't be easy. But the Scriptures pointed to the conquering attitude God wanted for me. "If anyone serves, he should do it with the strength God provides, so that in all things God may be praised through Jesus Christ" (1 Peter 4:11).

I'll never forget trudging up to the Sneads' house that freezing afternoon. Gripping Karen's hand, I stepped over the slick spots. Pausing at the door, I prayed for God's blessing upon the visit. But I still wondered, *Was I following God's leading, or was I foolish to go out in such treacherous weather?*

Mr. Snead beamed when he saw Karen and me, but he seemed worn and tense. A few minutes later, he pushed his wife's wheelchair into the room.

The couple delighted in our conversation, and they obviously loved watching Karen play with toys. They seemed to savor this Friday afternoon visit. As we prepared to leave, I prayed with them. I thanked God for Jesus and for the Sneads. Finally I asked his blessing on their Christmas.

Sunday morning brought a shock. Our pastor announced that on Saturday, Mr. Snead had died suddenly of a heart attack. I was stunned. But I knew then that God had guided me to visit them—on the day before Mr. Snead went to his heavenly home.

That winter day was a turning point for me. Since then, I've been ending my "appointment with God" with a follow-up listening and planning period. I listen for God's leading and I list each task or goal on a slip of paper the size of an index card. Then I prayerfully stack them in prioritized order.

I no longer keep long, overwhelming lists. Focused on the Lord, I am able to carry out one activity at a time. Some things get saved for another day. In the long run, I have more opportunities for meaningful service in my home or other situations where the Lord might want me. It's a rich adventure in Christ. And I'm learning that the best shortcuts to service begin with my morning meeting— just with him.

WORDS OF WISDOM

Presumptuous prayer speaks to God without first listening to him. It obsessively, anxiously, or pretentiously multiplies human words to God, but with, at best, a distracted, indifferent, or fitful interest in God's words to us. But God speaks to us before we speak to him. If we pray without listening, we pray out of context.

Eugene H. Peterson

GOD'S PROMISE

Listen to advice and accept instruction,
    and in the end you will be wise.

Proverbs 19:20

PRAYER

O Lord, I believe that you have a personal plan for my life that will affect the world around me for you if I will daily spend time with you in prayer and diligently look for you and listen to you through your Word and Spirit. Cause me to meet with you every day in a regular appointment for the rest of my life. Fill me with your Holy Spirit, woo me to your Word, increase my faith, and develop within me an incredible love for you. I ask these things in Jesus' name. Amen.

Becky Tirabassi

GOD'S VOICE AND A FULL TANK

Kathleen Swartz McQuaig

GOD'S WORD

Listen and hear my voice;
> pay attention and hear what I say.

Isaiah 28:23

"WHERE ARE WE GOING?" my children asked as I turned the car around. What reasonable explanation could I give them? I'd just exited the shopping area's parking lot, only to head back in again. I was as puzzled as they were.

Moments before, piling into our sun-baked car, a thought crossed my mind. Go, get gas. Glancing at the gas station across the parking lot and then at the gas gauge, I shook my head. The needle pointed to full—we didn't need gas. Hot and tired, we had turned for home; yet, so persistent was the thought that I found myself turning around.

"So where are we going?" my children asked again as we pulled back through the entrance.

"I have a strange feeling . . . that . . . we're supposed to get gas," I answered. "We don't need any, but I guess I can top off the tank."

Okay, Lord, I prayed as I finished pumping a few drops into my tank, I'm here; I don't know why, but I'm here.

I'd already paid for my gas and was heading back to our car when a woman with dark sunglasses reached for my arm. "You've got to pray for me," she blurted out. From behind her sunglasses, tears trickled down her cheeks. "I know you don't know me well, but I've seen you in church . . . and I really need you to pray for me."

Somewhere amidst her sharing, we moved our vehicles away from the pumps. Together we stood on the macadam between car doors while she poured her heart out. Though I invited her back home to talk, she seemed content with the compassion of the moment, open ears, and a simple promise of prayer.

As I hugged her goodbye she climbed back into the driver's seat and looked at

me intently. "I prayed for God to send me someone to talk to—you were his answer."

And to think I could have just gone home instead!

In a matter of weeks her situation was resolved, but for those few moments she needed to know that our Lord had heard her prayer. And I was reminded that our heavenly Father has the most accurate gauge of all.

GOD'S PROMISE

Jesus said, "My sheep listen to my voice; I know them, and they follow me. I give them eternal life, and they shall never perish; no one can snatch them out of my hand."

John 10:27–28

WORDS OF WISDOM

When I say that the Lord has spoken to me, I
mean something even more specific than general
revelation or private inner impressions. I reserve
these words intentionally for the rare, special
occasions when, in my spirit, I have had the Lord
speak directly to me. I do not mean, "I felt
impressed," or "I sensed somehow." Instead, I
mean that at a given moment, almost always
when I have least expected it, the Lord spoke
words to me. Those words have been so distinct
that I feel virtually able to say, "And I quote."

Jack Hayford

PRAYER

Lord Jesus, you were ever ready to listen to
those who cried out to you. You gave us ears to
hear: help us to hear. May we listen to all we
meet, and to those who come to us in trouble.
Remind us daily that there is a time for silence
and a time for speaking, and show us when to
speak and when to hold our peace. Never let us
miss a cry for help, because we are too busy
talking about ourselves. Make us ready to listen
to others, because we listen each day in silence to
you, O Jesus Christ our Lord. Amen.

Michael John Radford Counsell

God works with words. He uses them to make a story of salvation. He pulls us into the story. When we believe, we become willing participants in the plot. We can do this reluctantly and minimally, going through the motions; or we can do it recklessly and robustly, throwing ourselves into the relationships and actions. When we do this, we pray. We practice the words and phrases that make us fluent in the conversation that is at the center of the story. We develop the free responses that answer to the creating word of God in and around us that is making a salvation story.

EUGENE H. PETERSON

PRAYER
that
SAVES

Everyone who calls on the name of the LORD will be saved.

Joel 2:32

LETTING GO
Jim Cymbala

GOD'S WORD

> Oh, what joy for those
>> whose rebellion is forgiven,
>> whose sin is put out of sight!
> Yes, what joy for those
>> whose record the LORD has cleared of sin,
>> whose lives are lived in complete honesty!

Psalm 32:1–2 (NL)

ALL MY TALKING about prayer faced a severe test several years ago when Carol and I went through the darkest two–and–a–half–year tunnel we could imagine.

Our oldest daughter, Chrissy, had been a model child growing up. But around age sixteen she started to stray. Chrissy not only drew away from us, but also away from God. In time, she even left our home. There were many nights when we had no idea where she was. As the situation grew more serious, I tried everything. I begged, I pleaded, I scolded, I argued, I tried to control her with money. Nothing worked; she just hardened more and more. Her boyfriend was everything we did not want for our child.

Then one November, I was alone in Florida when I received a call from a minister whom I had persuaded Chrissy to talk to. "Jim," he said, "I love you and your wife, but the truth of the matter is, Chrissy's going to do what Chrissy's going to do. You don't really have much choice, now that she's eighteen. She's determined. You're going to have to accept whatever she decides."

I hung up the phone. Something very deep within me began to cry out. "Never! I will never accept Chrissy being away from you, Lord!" God strongly impressed me to stop crying, screaming, or talking to anyone else about Chrissy. I was to converse with no one but God. I was just to believe and obey what I had preached so often—"Call upon me in the day of trouble, and I will answer you." I dissolved in a flood of tears. I knew I had to let go of this situation.

I began to pray with an intensity and growing faith as never before. Whatever bad news I would receive about Chrissy, I kept interceding and actually began praising God for what I knew he would do soon.

February came. One cold Tuesday night during prayer meeting, I talked from Acts 4 about the church boldly calling on God in the face of persecution. We entered into a time of prayer, everyone reaching out to the Lord simultaneously.

An usher handed me a note. A young woman whom I felt to be spiritually sensitive had written: "Pastor Cymbala, I feel impressed that we should stop the meeting and all pray for your daughter."

I hesitated. Was it right to change the flow of the service and focus on my personal need?

Yet something in the note seemed to ring true. In a few minutes I picked up a microphone and told the congregation what had just happened. "The truth of the matter," I said, "although I haven't talked much about it, is that my daughter is very far from God these days. She thinks up is down, and down is up; dark is light, and light is dark. But I know God can break through to her, and so I'm going to ask Pastor Boekstaaf to lead us in praying for Chrissy. Let's all join hands across the sanctuary."

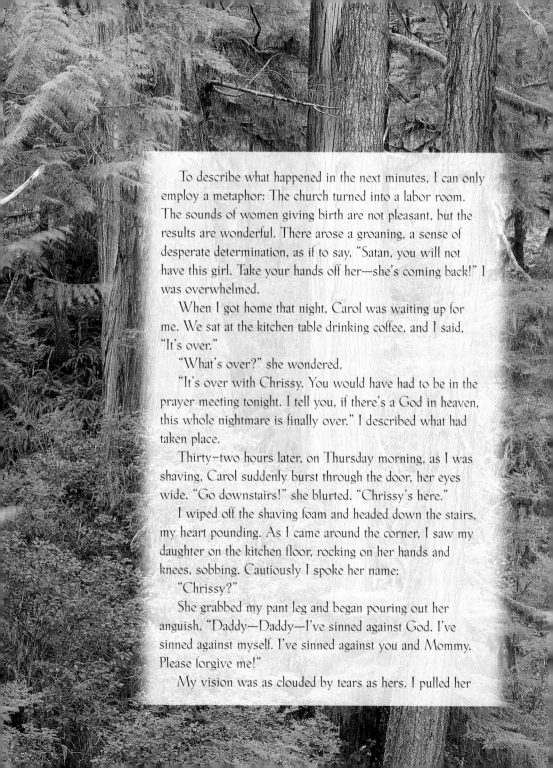

To describe what happened in the next minutes, I can only employ a metaphor: The church turned into a labor room. The sounds of women giving birth are not pleasant, but the results are wonderful. There arose a groaning, a sense of desperate determination, as if to say, "Satan, you will not have this girl. Take your hands off her—she's coming back!" I was overwhelmed.

When I got home that night, Carol was waiting up for me. We sat at the kitchen table drinking coffee, and I said, "It's over."

"What's over?" she wondered.

"It's over with Chrissy. You would have had to be in the prayer meeting tonight. I tell you, if there's a God in heaven, this whole nightmare is finally over." I described what had taken place.

Thirty-two hours later, on Thursday morning, as I was shaving, Carol suddenly burst through the door, her eyes wide. "Go downstairs!" she blurted. "Chrissy's here."

I wiped off the shaving foam and headed down the stairs, my heart pounding. As I came around the corner, I saw my daughter on the kitchen floor, rocking on her hands and knees, sobbing. Cautiously I spoke her name:

"Chrissy?"

She grabbed my pant leg and began pouring out her anguish. "Daddy—Daddy—I've sinned against God. I've sinned against myself. I've sinned against you and Mommy. Please forgive me!"

My vision was as clouded by tears as hers. I pulled her

up from the floor and held her close as we cried together. Suddenly she drew back. "Daddy," she said with a start, "who was praying for me? Who was praying for me?" Her voice was like that of a cross-examining attorney.

"What do you mean, Chrissy?"

"On Tuesday night, Daddy—who was praying for me?" I didn't say anything, so she continued:

"In the middle of the night, God woke me and showed me I was heading toward this abyss. There was no bottom to it—it scared me to death. I was so frightened. I realized how hard I've been, how wrong, how rebellious.

"But at the same time, it was like God wrapped his arms around me and held me tight. He kept me from sliding any farther as he said, 'I still love you.'"

"Daddy, tell me the truth—who was praying for me Tuesday night?"

I looked into her bloodshot eyes, and once again I recognized the daughter we had raised.

Chrissy's return to the Lord became evident immediately. By that fall, God had opened a miraculous door for her to enroll at a Bible college, where she not only undertook studies but soon began directing music groups. Today she is a pastor's wife in the Midwest with three wonderful children. Through all this, Carol and I learned as never before that persistent calling upon the Lord breaks through every stronghold of the devil, for nothing is impossible with God.

GOD'S PROMISE

Jesus said, "I am the light of the world. Whoever follows me will never walk in darkness, but will have the light of life."

John 8:12

WORDS OF WISDOM

We need to love people first, unconditionally, and only then will we know how to pray for them. True intercessors know that they can do nothing to change anyone else. Only God changes people. Knowing this, intercessors abandon all need to exercise influence over others, and out of this abandonment true prayer is born.

If we wish to pray effectively for others, we will never hold their faults against them, never reject them for their failings. It is not that intercessors are unaware of people's faults—but they are even more aware of the real person beneath the faults, the perfect child of God inside the rough exterior, and this is the person they choose to relate to and pray for. They pray not so much for the outer shell to be corrected, but rather for the spirit within to be encouraged and strengthened. If change is to happen, it will happen from the inside out. People do not change when their knuckles are rapped but when their inner beings are flooded with light.

Mike Mason

PRAYER

Let thy love so warm our souls, O Lord, that we may gladly surrender ourselves with all we are and have unto thee. Let thy love fall as fire from heaven upon the altar of our hearts; teach us to guard it heedfully by continual devotion and quietness of mind, and to cherish with anxious care every spark of its holy flame, with which thy good Spirit would quicken us, so that neither height, nor depth, things present, nor things to come, may ever separate us therefrom.

Strengthen thou our souls, animate our cold hearts with thy warmth and tenderness, that we may no more live as in a dream, but walk before thee as pilgrims in earnest to reach their home. And grant us all at last to meet with thy holy saints before thy throne, and there rejoice in thy love. Amen.

Gerhard Tersteegen

AN INVITATION AWAY
Karen Fuller

GOD'S WORD

> I pray also that the eyes of your heart may be enlightened in order that you may know the hope to which God has called you, the riches of his glorious inheritance in the saints, and his incomparable great power for us who believe.
>
> *Ephesians 1:18–19*

I ALWAYS FELT ALONE. No matter what relationship I was in, no matter what guy I was dating, no matter how many friends I had, I felt alone. In every relationship, I would push someone to love me, then give him reasons not to. I sabotaged what I wanted. As much as I wanted to be loved, I felt I didn't deserve it. Again and again I found myself going through this endless, hopeless cycle. But then something happened that eventually changed everything about who I was and what I thought I wanted in life.

Over dinner one night I told my friend Kim about my fears and loneliness. Get this—she used to deal with this exact same stuff! Then she said something a little odd. She told me she was a Christian and she prayed to God daily. When she asked if she could include me in her prayers, I just about fell off my chair. I couldn't believe someone was actually going to spend time praying for me. I teased her about being religious, but inside I was touched.

I knew things were really getting bad when I accepted an invitation from Kim to take in a service at her church. After spending the last year of our friendship badgering, challenging and belittling her faith, I was surprised that she even asked me. Even more surprising, I heard myself agree to go.

I expected to watch some kind of 'touchy-feely-praise-the-Lord-oh-look-how-perfect-we-are' religious presentation, but I was stunned by what I encountered. It wasn't some freak show for religious fanatics. In fact, these people appeared completely normal. I sensed that some of them may have even had the same hang-ups, disappointments, and anxieties as me. Get out!

They talked about how a five-year-old girl named Grace had just been killed in an auto accident. I remember wondering, *How could God allow a little child like that to die? Especially a child from a family who prayed so hard to adopt her and who loved her so much?* Then I heard that the parents of this little girl still kept their faith in God. Even though this tragedy happened in their life, they continued to love Him—and they knew that He continued to love them.

That was difficult to swallow, but I realized something. I wanted that. This love they relied on and expected and believed in—this was the kind of love I had been looking for my whole life. I was convinced that night, during that service, that something or someone was calling directly to me. . . .

Wow. I ended up, months later, sitting in the church with Kim, crying, asking God to come into my life, accepting Jesus as my Lord and Savior. I was twenty-nine years old and I had never prayed before. It was amazing.

I didn't used to think there was a God, but now I know there is, because He has changed me! I'm learning to give up those relationship-destroying habits and God has begun to break that endless, hopeless cycle I've been in for so long. I still struggle, and I have a long way to go, but there's no denying the contentment I feel. When I finally understood what Jesus did for me, I chose to believe and open my heart to Him.

It scares me to think I might never have learned about how much Jesus loves me had my friend Kim not prayed for me and invited me to church. It was a risk she took—and I'm eternally grateful.

GOD'S PROMISE

For this is what the high and lofty One says—
    he who lives forever, whose name is holy:
"I live in a high and holy place,
    but also with him who is contrite and lowly in spirit,
to revive the spirit of the lowly
    and to revive the heart of the contrite."

Isaiah 57:15

WORDS OF WISDOM

As I see it, true prayer is neither mystical rapture nor ritual observance nor philosophical reflection: it is the outpouring of the soul before a living God, the crying to God "out of the depths." Such prayer can only be uttered by one convicted of sin by the grace of God and moved to confession by the spirit of God. True prayer is an encounter with the Holy Spirit in which we realize not only our creatureliness and guilt but also the joy of knowing that our sins are forgiven through the atoning death of the divine savior, Jesus Christ. In such an encounter, we are impelled not only to bow before God and seek his mercy but also to offer thanksgiving for grace that goes out to undeserving sinners.

Donald G. Bloesch

PRAYER

Lord Jesus, . . . I believe thou didst die to set me free, not only in the future, but now and here. I believe thou art stronger than sin, and that thou canst keep me, even me, in my extreme weakness, from falling in its snares or yielding obedience to its commands. And Lord, I am going to trust thee to keep me. I have tried keeping myself, and have failed, and failed, most grievously. I am absolutely helpless. So now I will trust thee. I give myself to thee. I keep back no reserves. Body, soul and spirit, I present myself to thee as a piece of clay, to be fashioned into anything thy love and thy wisdom shall choose. And now I am thine. I believe thou doest accept that which I present to thee; I believe that this poor, weak, foolish heart has been taken possession of by thee, and that thou hast even at this very moment begun to work in me to will and to do of thy good pleasure. I trust thee utterly, and I trust thee now.

Hannah Whitall Smith

HORT'S HOMECOMING

Bob Haslam

GOD'S WORD

Jesus said, "There is rejoicing in the presence of the angels of God over one sinner who repents."

Luke 15:10

HORT WAS HIS NAME. He had been raised in a Christian home. But during his growing up years he decided against accepting Christ as Savior. He returned from war duty claiming to be an atheist. Hort's godly father and mother had fasted and prayed for him for many years. With his final breath, in fact, the father had prayed for his erring son.

My father first heard Hort's story when he went to pastor a church in Burlington, Washington. From Hort's brother and sister, both members of the congregation, my father learned that Hort was terminally ill. When my father inquired where their brother lived, they quickly replied, "Oh, you mustn't go there. Hort hates preachers and has cursed more than one of them off his property."

Knowing that Hort's parents had prayed faithfully for him, Dad began to pray for God's guidance. He called the church to pray that God would open Hort's heart to the gospel. Following all that prayer, my father drove to Hort's home. When he knocked on the door, Hort's wife appeared. "I'm Reverend Haslam," my father announced. "May I see Hort?"

Leading my father to her husband's bedroom, she announced, "Hort, Reverend Haslam is here to see you." Hort's icy gaze met my father's smiling eyes.

Hort was engrossed in a Seattle baseball game. "What's the score?" Dad asked. Hort told him. My father was an avid baseball fan. He knew all the Seattle players and even the players on opposing teams. He could talk baseball. Quickly, Dad and Hort were immersed in discussion. Their common interest began to build a bond between them.

When the game ended, Dad left without offering to pray or talk about God, a fact that haunted him over the following weeks. Still, he felt he should have the

Lord's clear leading before approaching Hort with the gospel.

On subsequent visits, Dad made a practice of going only when a Seattle game was in progress. Always, he and Hort enthusiastically discussed the game and players. Their shared interest developed into a genuine friendship. Still, no mention was made of God. Meanwhile, Hort's physical condition worsened.

One evening, my dad went over to watch the ball game by Hort's bedside. When the game was over, Dad stood at the foot of the bed and quietly asked, "Hort, may I say a prayer for you?" Hort nodded. For the first time, Dad lifted his voice in prayer in Hort's presence. As he prayed, he entreated God for Hort's spiritual as well as physical needs.

As Dad left, Hort gripped his hand and said nothing. The foot was in the door. It was time to bombard heaven for a dying man who needed God. Dad called the church to redouble its prayers for Hort's salvation.

Hort's wife phoned my father with a message: "Reverend Haslam, Hort wants you to bring your midweek prayer service to our home. And please make sure Mrs. Swanson comes. Hort has something he wants to say to her."

I was there that night, an eleven-year-old boy watching wide-eyed as everyone crowded into the living and dining rooms of Hort's home, prayerfully and expectantly. Hort was propped up in a wheelchair, heavily covered with blankets.

My father began with a hymn and a prayer. Then Hort raised his hand to signal he wanted to speak. His first words were addressed to Mrs. Swanson. He [recalled] that many years ago, the last time he was ever in church for a visit, she told Hort she was praying for him. With tears streaming down his face, Hort asked Mrs. Swanson's forgiveness for swearing at her under his breath. With that confession made, Hort tearfully asked my father to pray for him that God would forgive his sins and come into his heart.

As my father prayed, so did everyone there that night, myself included. At the end of the prayer, there wasn't a dry eye as Hort lifted both hands as high as he could in victory, as if Seattle had just won the league championship.

That night, the prayers of Hort's parents, who had gone on to heaven, were poured out, along with the prayers of Mrs. Swanson and God's faithful, believing people in that church. Everyone said it was a miracle. Especially Hort.

Word quickly spread around town, even down to Hort's favorite bar. Hort, the atheist, had given his heart to God!

The Sunday after the prayer meeting, Hort was lovingly brought into the church in the wheelchair in which he had accepted Christ. As he sat before the altar, my father admitted him to membership in a church he had long despised.

The next day, Hort was hurried to a hospital in a nearby town. There, he went to meet the beloved Savior who had died for his sins.

A few days later, we gathered for Hort's funeral. The service was a celebration of the grace of God, who is faithful in answering prayer even to the end. No one doubted where Hort was that day. Prevailing prayer had won the victory.

WORDS OF WISDOM

In one of his last acts before death, Jesus forgave a thief dangling on a cross, knowing full well the thief had converted out of plain fear. That thief would never study the Bible, never attend synagogue or church, and never make amends to all those he had wronged. He simply said "Jesus, remember me," and Jesus promised, "Today you will be with me in paradise." It was another shocking reminder that grace does not depend on what we have done for God but rather what God has done for us.

Philip Yancey

GOD'S PROMISE

Because of his great love for us, God, who is rich in mercy, made us alive with Christ even when we were dead in transgressions—it is by grace you have been saved.

Ephesians 2:4–5

PRAYER

Bring us, O Lord God, at our last awakening into the house and gate of heaven, to enter into that gate and dwell in that house where there shall be no darkness nor dazzling but one equal light; no noise nor silence but one equal music; no fears nor hopes but one equal possession; no ends nor beginnings but one equal eternity, in the habitations of thy majesty and thy glory, for ever and ever. Amen.

John Donne

FOR EVIE AND ME
Norma Knapp

GOD'S WORD

No eye has seen, no ear has heard, no mind has conceived what God has prepared for those who love him.

1 Corinthians 2:9

THE CALL PIERCED MY DREAM: "Norma!" In that place between sleep and wakefulness I tried to determine from which it came.

"Norma!" The call was more insistent this time.

I sat up quickly. The room stunk, a haze of disinfectant and rubbing alcohol. The hospital.

The white flannel sheet wrapped around my feet as I struggled to free my legs. Evie.

My eyes adjusted to the darkness. I left the warmth of the flannel and stepped onto the cold floor. A shiver shot through me. I shuddered and wrapped my arms around myself.

"Yes, Evie. I'm right here, Sissy." I could see my sister leaning on her elbow, hanging onto the side rail. Her right hand was clawing at the infusion pole by her bed in an attempt for assistance.

Hope and expectation danced in her eyes. "Norma I need you to help me get to heaven," she pleaded in her soft, southern accent.

Studying her I contemplated all that had happened in such a short time. Three months ago Evie was the picture of health. Now her entire body showed signs of the cancer destroying her.

"I'm here, Sissy," I replied reassuringly as I peeled her hand from the side rail and took it into my own. She relaxed, let go of the pole, lay back and squeezed my hand with incredible strength. I stroked her face.

"Help me get to heaven," she repeated.

"Of course I will," tumbled from my mouth. *Oh, Lord, why did I say that?*

I folded my hands. "Let's ask God to help us."

"Please do," she responded confidently, wrapping her hands around mine. Her piercing, cobalt blue eyes followed me and seemed to peer into my soul. For a moment

I couldn't move.

Then my right foot encircled the leg of the wooden chair behind me and pulled it closer. As I sat down a shaft of light from the partly open doorway cast a line across Evie's face. *How beautiful you are, Sissy. My only Sissy is dying, Lord.* Tears burned my eyes. I felt a thickening in my throat, a constriction against my chest. Carefully I lowered the side rail and pulled my chair even closer. Evie's eyes continued to follow me. *What do I know about this?* I took a deep breath and blew it out slowly.

"Heavenly Father," my voice squeaked. I cleared my throat and started again. "Lord . . . my Sissy . . . ." *Oh Lord, stay right here with me.* "Evie just asked me to help her get to heaven." My voice cracked. *I can't do this.* "You heard. She is ready."

"I am," Evie whispered confidently.

"Heavenly Father, Evie wants to know how to get to heaven. I think she knows. She just needs reassurance. You know her better than anybody, Lord. You know her heart."

With the back of my hand I wiped the tears flowing down my cheeks. "I want you to know, Lord, how special she is, how she loves us. She knows her time has come, Lord. Wrap your arms around her, Lord. Find a way to let her know you are here, that you truly love her, that you will never leave her!"

Her eyes snapped to mine in a moment of true understanding.

Tears streamed down my face. I wanted to run from the room and bellow my pain, but I was riveted. "I don't understand what you're doing, Lord, but you are in charge. Amen."

The quietness of the room enveloped us. Neither of us moved for a long time. Then Evie wheezed. "You have the prettiest blue eyes in the whole world, Norma."

I gasped. No words came. I squeezed her hand. She kissed mine. Peeling back the covers I crawled into bed beside her. We curled next to each other like spoons. Just like when we were little. I wept in surprise realizing this prayer was not for her. It is for me.

WORDS OF WISDOM

When you received Jesus as your Savior, you began to live in two homes—earth and heaven. You were born the first time into your earthly family. Now you have been born again into the family of God. You are a citizen of both worlds.

Your new heavenly home is the biggest one. It is God's home. It is yours because you are united to Jesus and heaven is where he lives.

But we don't need to wait until we die to visit heaven. Prayer is the airline to our heavenly homeland. We walk heaven's streets and view its wonders each time we fellowship with the Lord.

Ben Jennings

GOD'S PROMISE

Our citizenship is in heaven. And we eagerly await a Savior from there, the Lord Jesus Christ, who, by the power that enables him to bring everything under his control, will transform our lowly bodies so that they will be like his glorious body.

Philippians 3:20–21

PRAYER

Oh great, incomprehensible God! You who are omnipotent! Be my Heaven, in which I may live with my new birth in Christ! Let my spirit be the lyre, harmony, and joy of the Holy Spirit; strike the chord of your newborn image within me. Lead my harmony into your divine Kingdom of Joy, into the great praise of God, into the wonders of your glory and majesty, and into the communion of the holy angelic harmony. Build within me the Holy City of Zion, in which we, as Christ's children, shall live in one community—Christ within us! I yield myself completely to you! Do with me as You will! Amen!

Jacob Boehme

All of us have had that veil removed

so that we can be mirrors that brightly

reflect the glory of the Lord. And as

the Spirit of the Lord works within us,

we become more and more like him

and reflect his glory even more.

2 CORINTHIANS 3:18 (NL)

PRAYER
that
TRANSFORMS

We are becoming who we will be—forever.

Dallas Willard

THE NIGHT MESSENGER

Katherine Yurchak

GOD'S WORD

> May the words of my mouth and the meditation of my heart
> be pleasing in your sight,
> O LORD, my Rock and my Redeemer.
>
> *Psalm 19:14*

NOTHING WAS RIGHT THAT NIGHT. The harder I tried to sleep, the more I lay awake. The slant of the hospital bed aggravated my chronic back problem, the pillow didn't fit the nape of my neck, my roommate's faint snoring sounded like bombardments in my head.

Suddenly a diminutive gray-haired nurse, making her rounds at three in the morning, appeared in the dim light beside my bed. With her chin resting on the rail that imprisoned me, she inquired softly, "What can I do for you?"

I grumbled aloud, "I can't sleep in this place."

The woman in white rearranged the disheveled sheets that were badly twisted around my body because of my ceaseless tossing and turning. While she tended to my needs, I continued my noisy complaints: "I haven't had a bit of rest. I'll be glad when I get out of here. Maybe I can leave tomorrow—if tomorrow ever comes."

The kindly figure passed her cool hand over my heated brow and whispered, "You should be practicing your alphabet prayers."

The softness of her voice came as a rebuke to my loud laments. Ashamed, I lowered my tone and asked, "What kind of praying is that?"

"Start with any Scripture verse you can think of that begins with the letter A," she said. "And if you can't remember a verse, use a Scriptural theme. It will work fine. Just keep praying until you've gone through the entire alphabet. Don't worry about finding Scripture for the letters X, Y, and Z—you'll be fast asleep by then."

Desperate for rest, I was ready to accept the peculiar prescription for my sleeplessness. And so I began with the only verse that came to mind.

A—"All things work together for good to those who love God" (Romans 8:28 KJV). Good? All things? My mind raced to discover whatever pleasantry it could conjure up about my hospital stay. I reasoned it was good that my husband was there when I collapsed. And even though a bad bout with the flu had dehydrated my body, I did have to admit that it was good we lived only five minutes away from the hospital. Getting immediate treatment had to be a plus. I whispered a faint "thank you" to the Lord. Even so, I desperately wanted tomorrow to arrive now.

B—"Be not afraid; only believe" (Mark 5:36 KJV). The verse, coming in alphabetical sequence as it did, startled me. I recalled that they were the words the Lord had spoken to the woman who had pressed through a crowd to reach for Christ's garment. Now Christ was speaking comfort to me through my alphabet prayer. It was no surprise, then, that a welcome invitation was offered which I accepted.

C—"Come unto me all ye who are weary and heavy laden and I will give you rest" (Matthew 11:28 KJV). As I lay back quietly, I became aware that I had never studied Scripture with the express purpose of committing passages to memory. Rather, over the years, my daily readings of the Word of God generally included the prayer that the Holy Spirit would stamp truth on my heart and in my mind. My prayer was heard.

D—"Do unto others as you would have others do unto you" (Luke 6:31 KJV).

E—"Every good and perfect gift is from above" (James 1:17 KJV).

F—"Fret not thyself because of evildoers" (Psalm 37:1 KJV).

G—"God is love" (1 John 4:8 KJV).

H—"Have faith in God" (Mark 11:22 KJV). As the verses presented themselves one after the other, I sensed that as I was extending myself in prayer toward God, God was communicating with me.

I—"In all thy ways acknowledge him and he will direct thy paths" (Proverbs 3:6 KJV). "Lord, my desire is to faithfully serve you," I whispered. "Please forgive my surly attitude to the messenger you sent to my room tonight."

My head was sinking comfortably into the folds of the pillow that by now had molded itself around my neck. My roommate was no longer snoring. A solemn stillness enveloped the space around me.

At long last, I was in a state of rest. In peace I prayed on. I dozed and awoke praying:

Q—"Quietness and confidence shall be your strength" (Isaiah 30:15 KJV).

The night nurse was right. While praying alphabetically, I had fallen into a deep sleep long before reaching the letter Z.

I was awakened by the clattering of dishes. Tomorrow had arrived. And soon the doctor brought news that I could go home and recuperate. Never had the rays of the morning sun shone so bright.

There are times, even in the comfort of my own bed, that sleep eludes me. But when distresses loom large in the darkness, I recall the night messenger and her cure for insomnia. I lie back on my pillow and speak Scripture to God. Praying the alphabet way, I've found, is another means of providing the faithfulness of the Lord in bringing rest to the weary.

WORDS OF WISDOM

When in reading Scripture you meet with a passage
that seems to give your heart a new motion toward
God, turn it into the form of a petition, and give it a
place in your prayers.

William Law

PRAYER

Help me, O Lord, to make a true use of all disappointments and calamities in this life, in such a way
that they may unite my heart more closely with thee.
Cause them to separate my affections from worldly
things and inspire my soul with more vigor in the
pursuit of true happiness. Until this temper of mind be
attained I can never enjoy any settled peace, much less
a calm serenity. . . .

Enable me to love thee, my God, with all my
heart, with all my mind, with all my strength; so to
love thee as to desire thee; so to desire thee as to be
uneasy without thee, without thy favor, without some
such resemblance to thee as my nature in this imper-
fect state can bear. Amen.

Susanna Wesley

GOD'S PROMISE

The law of the LORD is perfect,
    reviving the soul.
The decrees of the LORD are trustworthy,
    making wise the simple.
The commandments of the LORD are right,
    bringing joy to the heart.
The commands of the LORD are clear,
    giving insight to life.
Reverence for the LORD is pure,
    lasting forever.
The laws of the LORD are true;
    each one is fair.
They are more desirable than gold,
    even the finest gold.
They are sweeter than honey,
    even honey dripping from the comb.
They are a warning to those who hear them;
    there is great reward for those who obey them.

Psalm 19:7–11 (NL)

A Changed Heart

Author Unknown

God's Word

Create in me a pure heart, O God,
and renew a steadfast spirit within me.

Psalm 51:10

FOR YEARS I WORKED in the front office of our small school here in upstate New York. I was receptionist, attendance officer, computer user, and telephone operator. I was the first person people saw when they came through the door. And I loved my job.

In the next office was the principal's secretary. We—and I mean this quite literally—hated each other. Our hatred was like a festering sore, and it had gone on for four long years. Don't think I'm exaggerating; I'm not.

The hate I felt for her kept me from being peaceful. I'd go home at night and think up ways to "get even." This wasn't just me, either; it was mutual. How I despised her; she tried to prove I was inadequate, and I tried to prove she was incompetent. Our glares and leers kept up every minute of every day. Our boss, the school principal, threatened to fire us both if we didn't stop feuding.

I didn't want to be like this. I'm really not a bad person. But I became afraid that the Devil really had hold of me. I tried—and failed—to fight this scourge by myself.

One day on my way back to work from an errand, I decided to try something new—prayer. The conversation went like this, word for word (because I remember every bit of it, even today):

"I need help. I can't live with this hatred inside of me. I can't shake it away. I'm not vicious. But I can't do it alone. I'm not strong enough; only you can help me. I don't want to die with his hatred. I want peace. Please. I'm scared."

I began sobbing and cried all the way back to work that day, pleading in prayer for a miracle.

When I arrived in school, I went straight to my nemesis' office and said, "Hi." She said, "Good morning." There was no mean feeling. I looked right at

her and honestly felt no animosity. It was like being cured of cancer.

I had been relieved of this ugly hate. I was calm, happy. She could tell I had changed. And you know, she changed, too. Now we're friends. We often share lunch and joke about how we hated each other. I tell everyone who notices the difference that it was prayer that changed me. People in school say, "I see you two are speaking now." I answer, "You won't understand, but it's a miracle."

WORDS OF WISDOM

Kingdom praying and its efficacy is entirely a matter of the innermost heart's being totally open and honest before God. It is a resolute intent and clarity of mind into the flow of God's action. In apprenticeship to Jesus, this is one of the most important things we learn how to do. He teaches us how to be in prayer what we are in life and how to be in life what we are in prayer.

Dallas Willard

GOD'S PROMISE

"I will give you a new heart with new and right desires, and I will put a new spirit in you. I will take out your stony heart of sin and give you a new, obedient heart," says the LORD.

Ezekiel 36:26 (NL)

PRAYER

O Lord God, destroy and root out whatever the adversary plants in me, that with my sins destroyed you may sow understanding and good work in my mouth and heart; so that in act and in truth I may serve only you and know how to fulfill the commandments of Christ and to seek yourself. Give me memory, give me love, give me chastity, give me faith, give me all the things which you know belong to the profit of my soul. O Lord, work good in me, and provide me with what you know that I need. Amen.

Columbanus

TROUBLEMAKERS

Pam Vredevelt

GOD'S WORD

Jesus said, "If you are willing to listen, I say, love your enemies. Do good to those who hate you. Pray for the happiness of those who curse you. Pray for those who hurt you.

Luke 6:27–28 (NL)

WHEN KEN WAS in the seventh grade, he had problems with a bully who humiliated him daily. He tripped Ken in class, yanked his chair out from underneath him, shoved his head in the water fountain when he was getting a drink, and made caustic remarks about him to others.

Ken's peace-loving personality tolerated this mistreatment for weeks until one day he finally reached his limit. Bursting into the house after an awful day at school, he poured out his heart to his mother, Nancy, detailing everything the bully had done since school began.

Like any other conscientious mother, Nancy wanted to do whatever she could to help her son. Wrapping her arm around his shoulder she said, "Ken, for some reason this kid has set himself up as your enemy. We don't know why, but I believe we can do something about it."

Ken's discouraged face lit up with hope as he waited to hear her idea.

"We need to say some prayers for this kid," Nancy continued. "God tells us to pray for our enemies. I believe if we do what God says, He will help you." From that day forward, they closed their evenings by praying for the "mean kid" in the class.

As the weeks passed, the mistreatment gradually dwindled. Within two months, the two boys were sitting together on the bus as field trip partners. School ended and Ken didn't see much of the troublemaker over the summer. But the following fall, the boy and his mother stopped by Ken's home to buy a jacket Ken had outgrown. The moms chatted over a cup of tea in the kitchen while the boys played. During their conversation,

the other mother paused and with a twinkle of gratitude in her eyes told Nancy, "My son just thinks the world of Ken!"

Many years have passed since those nasty run-ins at school. Teachers and classes have come and gone. Several outgrown jackets hang in the back of both boys' closets. Ken never really understood why the bully chose to pick on him. But it doesn't matter. Today, the boys are in high school, and Ken's former bully is now his good friend. They may be as different as night and day, but that doesn't keep them from being pals. The other kids they spend time with don't understand their tight bond. Ken simply calls it a "God thing."

What started out a curse turned into a blessing. This former bully and his entire family visited the church Ken and Nancy attended and started a new and exciting relationship with God.

Now when Ken has a problem with a troublemaker, he comes home, vents his frustration, and then says, "Mom, he's just asking for it!"

Prayer, that is.

GOD'S PROMISE

If you love your neighbor, you will fulfill all the requirements of God's law. For the commandments . . . are all summed up in this one commandment: "Love your neighbor as yourself." Love does no wrong to anyone, so love satisfies all of God's requirements.

Romans 13:8–9 (NL)

WORDS OF WISDOM

To be in the presence of even the meanest, lowest, most repulsive specimen of humanity is still to be closer to God than when looking up into a starry sky or at a beautiful sunset. For we cannot really love a sunset; we can love only a person. God is love, and in coming to him, we cannot escape coming through people. There is no separation between the spiritual and the social. The way we feel about people is the way we feel about God, and the way we treat people is the way we treat God.

Mike Mason

PRAYER

Almighty and tender Lord Jesus Christ, just as I have asked you to love my friends so I ask the same for my enemies. You alone, Lord, are mighty. You alone are merciful. Whatever you make me desire for my enemies, give it to them. And give the same back to me. If I ever ask for them anything which is outside your perfect rule of love, whether through weakness, ignorance or malice, good Lord, do not give it to them and do not give it back to me. You who are the true light, lighten their darkness. You who are the whole truth, correct their errors, You who are the incarnate word, give life to their souls. Tender Lord Jesus, let me not be a stumbling block to them nor a rock of offense. My sin is sufficient to me, without harming others. I, a slave to sin, beg your mercy on my fellow slaves. Let them be reconciled with you, and through you reconciled to me.

Anselm

PEACE BUS
Barbara Graham

GOD'S WORD
God is not a God of disorder but of peace.

1 Corinthians 14:33

I WORK FOR THE SCHOOL transportation department as a substitute attendant on the special education buses. One week I was assigned to a bus transporting young adults aged fifteen to seventeen to a hospital that serves as a tight-security school. These kids couldn't attend public school because they were violent and harmful to themselves and others.

The first young man we picked up was so violent that a trained technician from the hospital rode along with him. He was separated from the others on the bus, and under no circumstances was he to be left alone. I was anxious about this assignment, wondering how I could hold up over a period of days. The previous attendant had been stabbed and another had been bitten by a six-foot, hundred-and-eighty-pound boy. Anything could, and did, set them off. On our morning route three boys jumped another boy. I was so glad when we reached the hospital.

To tell the truth, I didn't want to go back in the afternoon to take them home. But I prayed, and a Scripture came to mind: "I am sending you out like a sheep among wolves. Therefore be as shrewd as snakes and as innocent as doves" (Matthew 10:16). I went back to work early so I could pray over the bus—door, windows, and each seat. I prayed for calm, peace, and cooperation. When our bus driver arrived, I told her I had prayed that each student would have peace.

We arrived at the hospital grounds and loaded the students on the bus. Even before we pulled out, the most violent student fell asleep. Ten minutes later, another was asleep. Twenty minutes, thirty, fifty—more than an hour later there was still not a sound on the bus from any of them. No one seemed to move. There was definitely peace and calm, all right.

The driver was amazed. "They . . . they . . . were good!" she stammered.

Both of us were grateful for an answered prayer. It may not be the greatest miracle God ever performed, but it was the miracle we needed that day.

WORDS OF WISDOM

Jesus Christ says, "Pray." It looks stupid; but when we labor at prayer results happen all the time from his standpoint, because God creates something in answer to and by means of prayer that was not in existence before.

Oswald Chambers

GOD'S PROMISE

You will keep in perfect peace all who trust in you,
whose thoughts are fixed on you!

Isaiah 26:3 (NL)

STEPS TO PEACE WITH GOD

1. **RECOGNIZE GOD'S PLAN—PEACE AND LIFE**

   The message you have read in this book stresses that God loves you and wants you to experience His peace and life.

   The BIBLE says . . . *"For God loved the world so much that He gave His only Son, so that everyone who believes in Him may not die but have eternal life." John 3:16*

2. **REALIZE OUR PROBLEM—SEPARATION**

   People choose to disobey God and go their own way. This results in separation from God.

   The BIBLE says . . . *"Everyone has sinned and is far away from God's saving presence." Romans 3:23*

   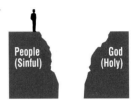

3. **RESPOND TO GOD'S REMEDY—CROSS OF CHRIST**

   God sent His Son to bridge the gap. Christ did this by paying the penalty of our sins when He died on the cross and rose from the grave.

   The BIBLE says . . . *"But God has shown us how much He loves us—it was while we were still sinners that Christ died for us!" Romans 5:8*

   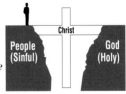

4. **RECEIVE GOD'S SON—LORD AND SAVIOR**

   You cross the bridge into God's family when you ask Christ to come into your life.

   The BIBLE says . . . *"Some, however, did receive Him and believed in Him; so He gave them the right to become God's children." John 1:12*

   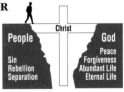

THE INVITATION IS TO:
REPENT (turn from your sins) and by faith RECEIVE Jesus Christ into your heart and life and follow Him in obedience as your Lord and Savior.

PRAYER OF COMMITMENT
"Lord Jesus, I know I am a sinner. I believe You died for my sins. Right now, I turn from my sins and open the door of my heart and life. I receive You as my personal Lord and Savior. Thank You for saving me now. Amen."

If you want further help in the decision you have made, write to:
Billy Graham Evangelistic Association, P.O. Box 1270, Charlotte, NC 28201-1270

If you are committing your life to Christ, please let us know! We would like to send you Bible study materials and a complimentary six-month subscription to *Decision* magazine to help you grow in your faith.

The Billy Graham Evangelistic Association exists to support the evangelistic ministry and calling of Billy Graham to take the message of Christ to all we can by every prudent means available to us.

Our desire is to introduce as many as we can to the person of Jesus Christ, so that they might experience His love and forgiveness.

Your prayers are the most important way to support us in this ministry. We are grateful for the dedicated prayer support we receive. We are also grateful for those that support us with contributions.

Giving can be a rewarding experience for you and for us at the Billy Graham Evangelistic Association (BGEA). Your gift gives you the satisfaction of supporting an organization that is actively involved in evangelism. Also, it is encouraging to us because part of our ministry is devoted to helping people like you discover and enjoy the stewardship of giving wisely and effectively.

Billy Graham Evangelistic Association
P.O. Box 1270
Charlotte, North Carolina 28201-1270
www.billygraham.org

Billy Graham Evangelistic Association of Canada
P.O. Box 2276 Stn M
Calgary, AB T2P 5M8
www.billygraham.ca

Toll free: 1-877-247-2426

ACKNOWLEDGEMENTS

The publisher has made every effort to trace the ownership of all quotations and to request the appropriate permissions. In the event of a question arising from the use of a quotation, we regret any error made and will be pleased to make the necessary correction in future editions of this book.

Adelsperger, Charlotte. "Visiting the Sneads," Originally published as "Prayer and Task Prioritizing," in the July/August 1998 issue of *Pray!* magazine. Used by permission of the author.

Anselm. Excerpted from *The Prayers and Meditations of Saint Anselm,* translated by Benedicta Ward SLG. Copyright 1973. Published by Penguin Books.

As told to Tom Sheridan. "A Changed Heart," Excerpted from *Small Miracles.* Copyright 1996 by Tom Sheridan. Used by permission of Zondervan Publishing House.

Askew, Eddie. Taken from *A Silence and a Shouting.* Copyright 1982. Published by The Leprosy Mission International.

Bernard of Clairvaux. Excerpted from *St. Bernard on the Christian Year,* translated by Sr. Penelope. Copyright 1954 by Community of St. Mary the Virgin. Published by A.R. Mowbray & Company.

Bloesch, Donald G.. Excerpted from *The Struggle of Prayer.* Copyright 1980 by Donald Bloesch. Used by permission of HarperCollins Publishers.

Boehme, Jacob. Excerpted from *The Way to Christ,* as quoted in *Companions for the Soul,* compiled by Robert R. Hudson and Shelley Townsend-Hudson. Copyright 1995 by Bob Hudson and Shelley Townsend-Hudson. Published by Zondervan Publishing House.

Calvin, John. *Institutes of the Christian Religion: Library of Christian Classics,* edited by John T. McNeill. Copyright 1960. Used by permission of Westminster John Knox Press.

Carmichael, Amy. Taken from *Amy Carmichael of Dohnavur* by Frank Houghton. Copyright 1988 by Frank Houghton. Used by permission of the Christian Literature Crusade.

Carney, Mary Lou. "The Late Commute," Originally published as the December 8 devotional in *Daily Guideposts 2000.* Copyright 1999 by Guideposts, Carmel, New York 10512. Reprinted with permission from *Daily Guideposts 2000.*

Chambers, Oswald. *My Utmost for His Highest.* Copyright 1963 by The Oswald Chambers Publications Association, Ltd. Published by Discovery House Publishers. *Workmen of God.* Copyright 1993 by The Oswald Chambers Publications Association, Ltd. Used by permission of Discovery House Publishers. All rights reserved.

Columbanus. Taken from *Celtic Christian Spirituality,* translated by Oliver Davies. Copyright 1995 by Oliver Davies. Used by permission of The Continuum Publishing Company.

Cook III, David C. Excerpted from "What Prayer Means to Me," in *We Believe in Prayer.* Copyright 1958 T.S. Dennison and Company.

Counsell, Michael John Radford. *2000 Years of Prayer.* Copyright 1999. Published by Morehouse Publishing.

Cymbala, Jim. *Fresh Wind, Fresh Fire.* Copyright 1997. Used by permission of Zondervan Publishing House.

Davis, James H. *Prayer in My Life,* edited by Sulon G. Ferree. Copyright 1967 The Upper Room. Used by permission of The Upper Room.

de Vinck, Christopher. *Simple Wonders.* Copyright 1995 by Christopher de Vinck. Used by permission of Zondervan Publishing House.

Dehquani-Tafti, Hassan. *A Procession of Prayers,* compiled by John Carden. Copyright 1998 by John Carden. Published by Morehouse Publishing.

Foster, Richard J. Excerpted from *Prayer.* Copyright 1992 by Richard J. Foster. Used by permission of HarperCollins Publishers.

Fuller, Karen, as told to Garry Poole. *The Three Habits of Highly Contagious Christians* by Garry Poole. Copyright 2000 by Willow Creek Community Church. Used by permission of Willow Creek Community Church.

Graham, Barbara as told to Quin Sherrer. *Miracles Happen When You Pray*. Copyright 1997 by Quin Sherrer. Used by permission of ZondervanPublishingHouse.

Graham, Billy. *Unto the Hills*. Copyright by Billy Graham. Used by permission of Word Publishers.

Gulley, Philip. *Front Porch Tales*. Copyright 1997 by Philip Gulley. Used by permission of Multnomah Publishers, Inc.

Hanford, William. "Kevin's Deliverance," Originally published as "Help My Unbelief!" in the January/February 2000 issue of *Pray!* magazine. Used by permission of the author.

Haslam, Bob. "Hort's Homecoming," Originally published as "Praying to the End," in the March/April 2000 issue of *Pray!* magazine. Used by permission of the author.

Hayford, Jack. *Glory on Your House*. Copyright 1982, 1991 by Jack Hayford. Published by Chosen Books.

Hilton, Ed as told to Quin Sherrer. *Miracles Happen When You Pray*. Copyright 1997 by Quin Sherrer. Used by permission of ZondervanPublishingHouse.

Hinkle, Lani Carroll. "Are You Listening?" Originally published in the July/August 1999 issue of *Pray!* magazine. Used by permission of the author.

Hobe, Phyllis. "Comfort One Another," Originally published as "Don't Hide Your Hurt," in *Daily Guideposts 1993*. Copyright 1993 by Guideposts, Carmel, New York 10512. Reprinted with permission from *Daily Guideposts 1993*.

Jennings, Ben. Excerpted from *The Arena of Prayer*. Copyright 1999 by Ben Jennings. Published by NewLife2000 Publications.

Jones, E. Stanley. Quoted in *Prayer Is*, compiled by William Arthur Ward. Copyright 1969 William Arthur Ward. Published by Droke House Publishers.

Keay, Kathy. *Laughter, Silence and Shouting*. Copyright 1994 by Kathy Keay. Used by permission of HarperCollins Publishers.

Knapp, Norma. "For Evie and Me," Originally published as "At Unexpected Times," in the May/June 1996 issue of *Virtue* magazine.

Lucado, Max. *The Great House of God*. Copyright 1996 by Max Lucado. Published by Word Publishing.

Marshall, Catherine. *Adventures in Prayer*. Copyright 1996. Published by Chosen Books.

Marshall, Peter. *The Prayers of Peter Marshall*, edited by Catherine Marshall. Copyright 1989 by Peter Marshall. Published by Chosen Books.

Mason, Mike. *Practicing the Presence of People*. Copyright 1999 by Mike Mason. Used by permission of WaterBrook Press, Colorado Springs, CO. All rights reserved.

Maynard, Lee "Wilderness Prayer," Originally published in the April 1998 issue of *Reader's Digest*.

McQuaig, Kathleen Swartz. "God's Voice and a Full Tank," Originally published in the July/August 1999 issue of *Pray!* magazine. Used by permission of the author.

Nappa, Mike. *True Stories of Answered Prayer*. Copyright 1999 by Nappaland Communication, Inc. Used by permission of Tyndale House Publishers. All rights reserved.

Nouwen, Henri J.M. with Donald McNeill and Douglas Morrison. Excerpted from "Compassion: The Core of Spiritual Leadership." Originally published in the January 1977 issue of *Worship Jubilee* 51. *Making All Things New* by Henri J.M. Nouwen. Copyright 1986 by Henri J.M. Nouwen. Used by permission of HarperCollins Publishers.

Parrott, Leslie as told to Jan Johnson Struck. "The Best Gift," Originally published in the May/June 1999 issue of *Today's Christian Woman* magazine.

Peterson, Eugene H. *Answering God.* Copyright 1989 by Eugene H. Peterson. Used by permission of HarperCollins Publishers.

Rowe, Elizabeth Singer. Taken from *Devout Exercises of the Heart,* as quoted in *Companions for the Soul,* compiled by Robert R. Hudson and Shelley Townsend–Hudson. Copyright 1995 by Bob Hudson and Shelley Townsend–Hudson. Published by Zondervan Publishing House.

Shoemaker, Samuel M. *We Believe in Prayer.* Copyright 1958 T.S. Dennison and Company.

Smith, Hannah Whitall. *The Christian's Secret of a Happy Life.* Copyright 1985 by Hannah Whitall Smith. Published by Fleming H. Revell.

Smith–Morris, Jennifer "Brady's Birthday," Originally published as "Prayer that Provides," in the June 1998 issue of *The Covenant Companion* magazine. Used by permission of the author.

Source unknown, quoted in *The Complete Book of Christian Prayer.* Copyright 1995 SPCK. Published in 1998 in the USA by The Continuum Publishing Company.

Spangler, Ann. Excerpted from *A Miracle a Day.* Copyright 1996 Ann Spangler. Used by permission of Zondervan Publishing House.

Strand, Karen. "God, Please Protect Jody," Originally published as "The Day I Learned to Pray," in the November/December 1998 issue of *Moody* magazine. Used by permission of the author.

Tada, Joni Eareckson. "A Prompting from the Spirit," Originally published in *Moody* magazine.

Taylor, Jeremy. Taken from *The Power of Prayer* by Samuel Irenaeus Prime, as quoted in *Companions for the Soul,* compiled by Robert R. Hudson and Shelley Townsend–Hudson. Copyright © 1995 by Bob Hudson and Shelley Townsend–Hudson. Published by Zondervan Publishing House.

Taylor, Margaret T. *Encounters: A Prayer Handbook.* Copyright 1998. Published by the United Reformed Church.

ten Boom, Corrie. Taken from *He Cares, He Comforts.* Copyright by Chosen Books.

Tersteegen, Gerhard. Quoted in *The Pietists,* edited by Peter Erb. Copyright 1983 by Peter Erb. Published by Paulist Press.

Tirabassi, Becky. Excerpted from *Let Prayer Change Your Life.* Copyright 1990, 1992, 2000 by Becky Tirabassi. Published by Thomas Nelson Publishers, Inc.

Vredevelt, Pam. *Espresso for Your Spirit.* Copyright 1999 by Pam Vredevelt. Used by permission of Multnomah Publishers, Inc.

Willard, Dallas. Excerpted from *The Divine Conspiracy.* Copyright 1998 by Dallas Willard. Used by permission of HarperCollins Publishers.

Yancey, Philip. *What's So Amazing about Grace?* Copyright 1997 by Philip Yancey. Used by permission of Zondervan Publishing House.

Yurchak, Katherine. "The Night Messenger," Originally published in the December 1999 issue of *Sacred Journey* magazine. Used by permission of the author.